SELLING OUT TO YOUR LEVEL OF COMFORT

Randy King

Selling Out to Your Level of Comfort

Copyright © 2017 Randy King. All rights reserved.

ISBN-13: 978-1542534826
ISBN-10: 1542534828

Printed by CreateSpace

All rights reserved. Without limiting the rights under the copyright reserved above, no part of this publication may be reproduced, stored in, or introduced into a retrieval system, or transmitted in any form or by any means (electronic, mechanical, photocopying, recording, or otherwise) without prior written permission of Randy King.

While every effort has been made to ensure the accuracy and legitimacy of the references, referrals, and links (collectively 'Links') presented in this book, Randy King is not responsible or liable for broken Links or missing or fallacious information at the Links. Any links to a specific product, process, website, or service do not constitute or imply an endorsement by Randy King of same, or its producer or provider. The views and opinions contained at any Links do not necessarily express or reflect those of Randy King.

Material in this book is for educational purposes only. This book is sold with the understanding that neither the publisher nor the author is engaged in rendering legal, financial, or any other professional service. Neither the publisher nor the author assume any liability for any errors or omissions or for how this book or its contents are used or interpreted or for any consequences resulting directly or indirectly from the use of this book. For legal, financial advice or any other, please consult the appropriate professionals.

For updates, new releases, useful links, and other information, check out:

http://randykinglive.com/

DEDICATION

This is dedicated to all the patient humans in my life that allow me to be the crazy workaholic that I am! Thank you to each and every one of you who have helped me succeed!

Oh and of course to my daughter Jasmine ... 'cause we can't let Rory be wrong ...

CONTENTS

Foreword by Rory Miller i
Preface iii

Part One: The Basics 1
   1 Introduction 3
   2 Why You? 9
        Worksheet 1 - Why You? 11
   3 Defining Your Brand 13
        Sample Yes/No/Maybe List 18
   4 Getting Started 19
        Worksheet 2 - Getting Started 23
   5 Red Tape 25
        Checklist 27
   6 Budgeting 29
   7 Goals 33
        Worksheet 3 - Goals 38
   8 Pricing Yourself 39
        Worksheet 4 - Pricing / Overhead Model 47

Part Two: Marketing and Sales 49
   9 Overview 51
  10 Traditional Marketing 55
  11 Internet Marketing and SEO 59
  12 Your Website 65
  13 How to Market with Social Media 69
        Example Social Media Marketing Plan 76
  14 Sales 81

Part Three: Longevity and Culture — 89

    15 Content Creation — 91

    16 Sponsoring Ads / What is PPC? — 97

    17 Being Allergic to Overhead — 101

    18 Knowing Who You Are — 107

           Worksheet 5 - Strengths / Weaknesses — 110

    19 Building Your Team — 111

    20 Creating a Culture — 115

    21 Keep Growing — 119

Further Reading — 121
About the Author — 123

FOREWORD

by Rory Miller[1]

I bet Randy's going to dedicate this book to his daughter. I want to dedicate it to some of the last generation of instructors. Extraordinary teachers who taught in their garages while just getting by on a pension. Or taught in their shitty section-eight apartments for cigarette money. Truly exceptional fighters who died in poverty. People who should have been household names but died (too often drinking themselves to death) in obscurity. They needed this book.

And, likely, so do you.

Martial artists have created a myth. We call the commercially successful training halls "McDojos" and worship the eccentric old man who teaches the good stuff to a handful of people in his garage. We have taught ourselves that there is an inverse correlation between skill and financial success. And that's bullshit. Worse, it's a destructive, pathetic, self-fulfilling prophecy.

Look at it this way: The world of business is just as much an arena as the mat, the octagon or the ring. It is a place with winners and

---

[1] http://chirontraining.com/

losers, an environment where skill, insight and heart are necessary to prevail. To enter that arena and refuse to learn how to prevail is stupid. It is not noble. It is not moral.

It is arrogance, and worse, it is the kind of arrogance that makes losers. What do you call someone who enters a grappling match but refuses to learn to grapple? A loser. And you laugh, because it is so obvious that only a moron could possibly...

So what do you call a martial arts instructor who opens a school and refuses to learn recruitment and retention, or pricing, or... "Well that's a master, of course. Far beyond trivial concerns like money..." Nope, still a loser. And a moron.

Here's the deal. Somewhere, on some level, if you are teaching martial arts or self-defense or damn near anything, you are teaching strategy. How to get things done. Nowhere and at no time has *"ignore the way the world works"* been a tenet of strategy. If you are a strategist and plan to pass that skill on to your students, what message do you send when you fail out of arrogance?

Once you open your doors to the public, you have a right and a responsibility not to suck. Randy's book will help you not suck. We've all been brainwashed that "selling out" is a necessary part of success. Randy proves it isn't. So buy this book. Read it. And don't suck. Your students are watching.

PREFACE

Well, I never thought I would be a writer, but here we are! Thanks so much for buying this book! I know it will be one of the best investments you make in your business and towards your personal growth. Too many amazing instructors are stuck teaching in their garages, because they have no idea what to do when it comes to getting their name out there. The old adage of "build it and they will come" is so stuck in most people's heads that when their business does not blow up within a month, they get disheartened and quit.

The information contained in this book will help you to start, grow, or renew your business, and also help you to weather the storms when they come. Although some people manage to make it look easy, in reality running a business is constant work, constant hustle. The second you get complacent is the second you start losing. The road you have chosen is not for the faint of heart, but in these pages I will give you the strategies you need to make your work more efficient, to start creating plans, and to do less "busy-work".

I want to teach you how to get back to doing what you love.

I am going to be giving a lot of examples, both to help make my points, and also to help you with filling out the worksheets. These examples are drawn from my own experiences and represent my personal views on business. I had a very specific vision of what I wanted to create. Take all my examples as just that, *examples* - they are not opinions or suggestions on what you should do for your business. If you get one thing out of this book, it should be that I want you to create your brand, not a copy of mine. When I bash kid's classes, or black belt clubs, I am not really suggesting that these are bad ideas - they are just not what I wanted for my business.

I would like to give a thank you to Rory Miller, who did everything short of putting a gun to my head to get me to write this book.

If this book helps you to create a better business, then I am pumped! Please get in touch and tell me, I would hate to miss out on your story! At the end of this book you will find my contact info; shoot me an email and tell me your experiences and thoughts, or if you have your own strategies you want to share, please tell me so I can spread the word!

Enjoy.

PART ONE

THE BASICS

1 INTRODUCTION

How do you start a book? I guess, better yet, how do you start a business? How do you start a book <u>about</u> business? I guess this way is as good as any! My name is Randy King, and I am here to tell you how to run your business!

Just kidding.

Right out of the gate, I want you to know that this is not a paint-by-numbers plan on how to run a business exactly like mine. It is meant as a reference book, containing tools, tricks, and questions, all of which will help you run the business you want to be running. Every person has different strengths, and if you try to create a copy of someone else's business, you will just end up with a poor copy. The point of this book is to show you how to build a business that will reflect who <u>you</u> are, and reflect <u>your</u> passions.

The title of this book is "Selling Out to Your Level of Comfort". What do I mean by that? A little background first. I've seen too many business owners open a business with the greatest of intentions. Through bad advice, shitty returns, bad clients, and/or bad business knowledge, they turn their dream into something they never wanted it to be. I've seen people turn luxury restaurants into fast food restaurants. Take a look at the McDonald's brothers, who just wanted to own a great restaurant. All of a sudden some guy came in and franchised the hell out of it … and now McDonald's is synonymous with junk food. This is common in many service-based businesses. You decide to open a gym because you were the best mixed martial artist of your time, and you really want to pass on what you think is important. At some point, maybe after a couple of bad months, you start looking to various gurus, and *senseis*, and businesspeople, who all say that they can have you making six figures ... if you just change everything about your business and make sure that you do it exactly like they do it. Sounds great ... until you realize your badass MMA vision has now turned into a cardio-kickboxing gym.

That is the whole reason I wrote this book. I want to help people realize the vision of their business that they have in their heads; not some copycat, watered-down version. This book can help you to create that business. One you can not only live off, but also be proud to own. One you can even build your retirement on.

Am I leading by example? Well, I haven't become rich yet myself, but I'm definitely on my way. I've made a promise to my eight-year-old daughter Jasmine that one day we will be rich. The methods in this book can definitely get you there ... but this is bootstrapping, not bullshit. It is going to take some work. If you are looking to get a grasp on your business, run a business that you love and that you will actually be proud of, and not have to do the things you don't want to do, and not sell out, then this is the book for you.

So, why "selling out to your level of comfort"? Well to each person "selling out" looks totally different. What you consider to be selling out might be someone else's plan A. Do I want you to "sell out"? YES ... but only in ways that don't make you sick. I hope this book gives you some new ways of looking at things, and brings you some tools you might not have considered, but it will always stay up to you whether you take any of my advice. This is a realistic view of how to run a business in the client-based service industry, where your job is to create a group of people that come back over and over again, while you live your dream.

Seriously though, who the hell am I, and why would you read a book by somebody who just told you he's not going to make you instantly rich? Well, I am just a guy who loves to see people succeed. There are plenty of people out there willing to sell you their "get rich quick" plan, and they're not exactly lying; they will definitely get <u>themselves</u> rich (off of you - just talk to them and send them money for their course!).

I actually started my current business, KPC Self Defense, by accident - I did not want to start a business! I loved <u>training</u>, but to me, instructing was for old people - it was what you did once you'd finished doing all the cool things you could, when all you had left was to give back through teaching. I had just gone through a divorce, was working for an advertising firm and doing really well - I've always been told by people that I'm very friendly and charismatic, a natural sales person, 'the closer'. I really liked it, liked the competition of it. I had also come off of a couple of head injuries, and I couldn't fight competitively anymore, so I had to get my sense of a "win" from somewhere else. The shark tank of sales and advertising really fed my ego and made me feel better. (If KPC fell apart tomorrow - if all of this "living the dream" and travelling around the world, meeting people far cooler than me and helping them grow their businesses - if that all failed, I would definitely go right back into advertising.) I have always treated everything in my life as a competition; most of you probably get that, so when I say I was the best, it wasn't just talent. We all know hard work beats talent when talent does not work hard. So of course there was a lot of hard work and training involved, just like anything in life.

One day I was driving back to Edmonton with my best friend Chris Jimmo and my now-business partner Thor. We had just attended a seminar in Calgary with one of my mentors, Professor Kelly Worden[2] (I highly recommend checking out his training if you're into knife stuff.) I was going through a rough time, and Professor Worden and I had had an awesome talk. He had also gone through a divorce, and he was trying to get me back on track, as he does; he cares a lot about his students.

---

[2] http://kellyworden.com/

As we were driving and talking, I said "Man ... one day I want to do what Professor does", so Thor asked "why not just open a gym?" My first reaction was to say "no, I can't open a gym; I can't take the risk!" I only had a small group of about ten to fifteen people who were training with me on weekends, and most of the time I didn't even charge. The only reason I started charging was due to the fact that people wouldn't come otherwise. Thor then so cleverly pointed out that we had about ten people training regularly, and if everybody paid, we could maybe pull it off. Chris (who gives me the best ideas, you should probably be reading a book by him) did some quick math and told me, "Look, if you get your eight to ten students to pay for a year up front, at a low fee, that will probably pay opening costs."

Right there is where KPC was born. I had no idea that car ride would change my life so much.

So, after being outwitted by my friends, I started down this road. I made the choice that I wanted to create my own vision of what a gym should be like. I had many friends at the time telling me not to do it. People told me I was crazy to leave a well-paying job to open a fight club in the ghetto. Some of those people had even run clubs of their own and failed. Though once I had made up my mind, none of that ever bothered me. I knew what I wanted and I went for it; I did it my way, and here we are today.

I found a place within our price range, and that place was in a shitty part of town. Luckily, the martial arts legend exists that people need to be in crappy places to train, that's where all the good martial arts are done, right? In Mr. Miyagi's workshop, in the old abandoned MMA gym from "Never Back Down", in the train yard, etc. As luck would have it, the brand I was trying to build was actually helped out by the whole idea that we were in a junky location. People will come to bad places for good service. (Where is the best Chinese food? Not at the mall!) Plus, being in this location allowed us to grow very quickly, so we could end up in a great part of town like we are now.

Next, it was time for planning. I am huge fan of plans and you should be too! We crushed our five-year plan in under two years.

We hit a huge stride, worked nonstop, and I never gave up on our dream. Every bit of advice I got, if I didn't like it I just passed it by, and stayed true to my vision. I didn't care about how amazing it sounded (kid's classes for example). If it didn't fit with my vision, I didn't go for it. This is so important. Never let those who can't, get in the way of those that are.

KPC is now in its ninth year of business. I have been teaching full-time for seven years. Plus I now travel around the world teaching others my brand of self-defense. Some consider me successful because I only teach what I want, when I want, to whom I want, and I can still make a good living at it. For me, however, this is still a work in progress, and as you will read later, I measure success a little differently than most. That being said, if you are in, I am willing to share what I did to get here.

Let's get started.

2 WHY YOU?

Let's start off by asking some hard questions. First up, why you? Why do <u>you</u> have to be the one opening a new business? What special gifts or tricks or talents do you possess that makes the world so in need of your service? This may sound harsh, but it is a cruel reality. Why should I come and buy a service from you, when I can go and get the same damn thing from an established business?

During every business talk I have with gym owners, I ask this very important question. Can you name me five things right now that make you different than your competition down the street? If your first answer is "price", right there you have lost this war. There have to be reasons why you opened your own business. There is a reason you didn't buy a franchise. So why you? Answering this question will be easy for some and very hard for others, but if you can't give me five reasons (outside of price) why I should use <u>your</u> service, it is going to be very hard for you to get clients. Hell, it will be hard to even make your business sound interesting at parties.

I want you to think long and hard on those five things, then fill out the worksheet at the end of this chapter. This will start you on the path to making your business stand out, and it will make things easier when it comes to marketing. The first thing that you put on that list will most likely become your message, and it will be the single thread that ties all of your efforts together.

I'm going to ask you to decide who, what, and where you want to teach, and why you want to do it. Just like with those first five things I asked you to list, I want you to get specific in your answers to these questions. Don't answer with generalities like "I want to teach everybody"; that is too broad and will not help you at all. And if the only reason you want to do it is to make a lot of money ... then get into banking, or go to law school, or become a doctor. Invest, design a product, create the next SlapChop. Products make more money than services; they always will.

I want you to sell out to your level of comfort. These questions will find where that comfort level is, and throughout the first part of this book we will be defining and testing that level.

Worksheet 1 - Why You?

Name five things that make your business unique:

1.

2.

3.

4.

5.

Who do I want as clients?

What do I want my service to provide?

Where do I want to provide this service (from home, in a gym, at a mall)?

Why you?

3 DEFINING YOUR BRAND

What is driving you to take the hardest possible path? If you wanted to open your own business, you could easily just go online, find a franchise, and get all the information you need to run your own gym under their banner. You could certify under somebody else, open a gym under their name, pay them their dues, and become pretty successful. That would be the easy way out! It sounds great, doesn't it? And it always will. But it will never be *your* gym, *your* vision, *your* brand.

You need to love your brand, be confident that no one can do it like you. Your brand will even become you. Your brand will become the entire identity of the business so you need to define it very clearly.

Knowing what you are good at is a powerful tool. Everyone loves working with a specialist. They love bragging about how much their provider knows. Knowing who reacts best to you is also very powerful. Once you've identified the niche for your brand, you can focus all your research and marketing on the people most likely to invest in your services. That is a huge tool that not many people take advantage of. You need to know what your standard is and stick to it. Don't get caught up jumping on fads and relying on pop culture to define who you are. If you stick to your message you will do well.

In order to define your brand, you need to make another list (see the sample at the end of this chapter). This list will consist of three columns. The first column will be the "yes" column - all the things you want to do in your business that make you stand out from everybody else. The second column is for "maybes" - things you've never considered doing or haven't done before, but are not directly opposed to. The third column is for the "never" items - things you would absolutely never even consider doing.

Be specific. Don't write "make money and pay bills", either. You want to establish the identity of your business here.

If you are having trouble filling out your list, don't worry. It happens. Things for your "maybe" list can be particularly tricky to pin down. If you're stuck, then it's time for some research. Look around at what businesses in your field are doing all over the world, write down what their tactics are, and see where they fall on your list.

There's a sample worksheet at the end of the chapter, with my "yes", "maybe", and "never" lists for KPC. I'll be using KPC as my example in this book a lot, not because I want to keep pumping KPC into your brain (we'll talk about that later!) but because it is the business that I'm running right now, and these are actual examples of my process. Remember that these are not suggestions for you to follow - they are just examples to get your juices flowing. Copying my ideas won't get you any nearer to your goal than copying anyone else's.

The "yes" column is for all the things you want to do that will make you different. I wanted KPC to be a reality-based self-defense gym, where the head instructor's word is not law and can be challenged. I did not want a formal gym. I wanted to be teaching up-to-date, practical material, in a fun, safe environment. I also wanted to reward long-term students - as a person who had trained at multiple martial arts gyms, I was sick of getting charged more money the longer I stayed. These were the things that made me want to open my own gym, because no gym like this existed in my area. Completing the "yes" column should be easiest.

In the "never" column, I listed the things I didn't want to ever do. I never wanted to run a kid's class. I never wanted to have a black belt club. No MMA fighters - we helped people compete for a bit, but I honestly didn't have the stomach to watch my students fight without wanting to help. Knowing who you are helps a lot in business; the more you know yourself, the more pure your brand will be. After drawing these lines in the sand, I had a much better idea of what I needed to create. The points in the "never" column are non-negotiable. Unless something drastic changes, the "never" column is off-limits … that is the beauty of this system. Knowing what you hate right off the bat will help you make better choices. I will never give you the advice to try something on your "never" list. The second you do, the business is no longer what you wanted. Tiny concessions destroy legacies. For me, a big "never" was any type of Black Belt Club (BBC). Every other book you read is going to tell you that paying for "special classes" is the best way to go - charging already-existing loyal clients more money is smart, they will pay! I agree that this is a *smart* tactic, but I am just not a fan. Should *you* do a BBC? If you're ok with them, do them! This is not me trying to talk you out of having a BBC at your gym, they simply represent a line I will not cross. There are many ways to win in this game, and you need to find yours.

The trickiest column is the "maybe" column; the things you haven't tried yet but that you are not against. This is by far the most important column for you to expand on and define your brand. In my own "maybe" column, the big standout was curriculum.

For the first three years at KPC, we had no working curriculum. Curriculum is a huge thing that almost all martial arts gyms do. I wasn't against having a curriculum, in theory - I was more against the idea of a curriculum that plotted a fixed course of "this move leads to this move". So, instead of a fixed curriculum, I just taught what I wanted. I would look at what felt relevant at the time. It might have been something a student had asked about, something I had trained at a seminar, something I wanted to work on, something I'd seen in the UFC - anything I thought my group should know. That was fine for us for three years.

As I started traveling more with my seminar circuit, my assistant instructors were having trouble with my teach-on-the-fly model because, oddly enough, they aren't me! I was running into what is called the "dentist problem". (You're going to run into this a lot, if you are the operating entrepreneur. If you're a really good dentist, then everybody wants you and only you; even if you tell them other dentists are also really good, they'll still wait for you.) If I wasn't at the gym, people wouldn't come to classes. When I was in the Philippines training, and I had my instructors running the gym, student numbers went down. (We also ran into another interesting problem, which was that some people who signed up while I was away could not stand me when I came back, as they preferred Thor's teaching style.)

Once I gave some thought to my "maybe" column, and having seen the drawbacks of working without a curriculum, I decided that I would set a curriculum, but do it my own way. What resulted was a self-defense-focused curriculum, based on the books "Scaling Force: Dynamic Decision Making Under Threat of Violence"[3], by Rory Miller and Lawrence Kane, and "Facing Violence: Preparing for the Unexpected"[4], by Rory Miller. I didn't make the decision to add a curriculum in order to make money, or because I was trying to make the business bigger. I made the decision because after reading Rory's books, I had way too much information that I wanted to convey to my students, and there was no way any of the instructors could teach all the material without a structured curriculum to follow.

Today's KPC was born from that middle column. Implementing the curriculum made us explode. All of a sudden, the levels that we had at KPC made way more sense, and fit together better, and clients responded very well to that. We needed testing, to ensure people got through the levels safely, and to find out what they were capable of, so I introduced standard tests, but made them free and called them assessments. This one little thing that I never

---

[3] https://www.amazon.ca/Scaling-Force-Dynamic-Decision-Violence/dp/1594392501/
[4] https://www.amazon.ca/Facing-Violence-Unexpected-Rory-Miller/dp/1594392137/

cared about not only became the backbone of my business, but helped us get to the next level. The most growth I have ever seen in businesses has stemmed from trying things in that middle column without compromising on anything in the "never" column.

Once you've written out your three columns, you can take a good look at them and use them to decide where to go next.

The "yes" column is the easiest to act upon; just get on it and do those things! These are the items that will make your brand stand out. The middle ground - the maybes - are the things that I want you to try that might change your thought process, and might blow up and make things amazing! Finally, the "never" list. These are the lines I don't want you to cross. I don't care what some super-rich shiny white-toothed good-looking f@$&er says on YouTube - if you don't want to do something - DON'T DO IT. Too many amazing projects have shut their doors because their business turned into something they didn't want and didn't recognize.

Once you've completed your list, you know what makes you, you. You know what you want to accomplish, and you also know what you will never do.

Now what?

Sample YES/MAYBE/NEVER list (KPC)

YES	MAYBE	NEVER
informal	curriculum	kid's classes
reality based, no-nonsense	ladies-only classes	black belt club
fun, safe environment	schools	mandatory anything
rewarded for training longer	contracts	bandwagon jump

4 GETTING STARTED

"How do I start a gym" is probably the biggest question I get all the time, and there is no simple answer.

There are hundreds of thousands of Facebook memes saying that people will doubt you until you are successful, and then they will ask you how you did it. Those memes are true. Many people in your support structure will be against what you are trying to do. This is exactly what happened with KPC. Until things started to look good, most of my friends were doubtful that my idea would work, and they weren't shy about saying so! For a while, I couldn't prove them wrong. But I would much rather do something I love; and if you are on this path, then obviously so would you. This is a career of passion, not a job filled with instant profits. Ideally you'll achieve both, with some old-fashioned hustle and grind. Until you have something to show for your work, though, the people around you will be skeptical.

Now that you know what makes you different and what unique service you can offer your customers, it's time to delve deeper into those questions you answered on Worksheet 1. What is your message? Who do you want to teach? How do you want to do it?

What exactly is a "message"? Your message is what you are putting out there. A great example of a group with a very clear message is any charity. They all have a very specific message, focused on the cause they are helping out with. Everything they do with their charity, from marketing to website to networking to photo shoots, all revolves around their cause. You need to do the same thing with your business. You need to create a unique message, and then everything going forward needs to stay on that message. From branding to cross-promotions, the message is key!

How do you decide what your message is? Simple - take the major thing that makes you different, and then make that very specific. It is the answer to the "why you?" question. Your message is by far the most important part of your business. Everything from this point forward should be revolving around your message.

The next thing you will need to decide on is your demographic, the group you want to attract. This is essential in order to focus your efforts, plus it keeps advertising costs down. When you are starting a business, low costs are good.

When I ask you to pick a demographic I want you to be super specific ... starting to see a trend here? Just saying fifteen- to twenty-five-year-old males is not good enough. I want you to know the exact type of people that either you specifically enjoy teaching, or those that respond best to you. I have seen businesses catering to all types of humans work - so if you want to be teaching fit young law enforcement, that is who you should target. The more specific your initial demographic, the faster you will get a core group of students. This will take some work, and it may change over time, but figuring this out is very important. Make sure your demographic links up with your message.

Last but not least, you need to establish how you envision your business looking. What medium will you be using to teach your students? We live in a time of wonders. Your product can be accessed in more ways than ever before! You could run classes or seminars in person or online. You could teach at your own location, or offer seminars and courses at third-party locations. Knowing the way you are going to be presenting will help you make future choices. It will also help you focus on where to invest time and money. For instance, I wish we had bought a camera earlier. You can clearly use multiple types of media, but it's better if you know that's what you're planning to do right out of the gate.

A major thing that ties into your message, and one of the most enjoyable parts of owning a business, is when you get to create your branding. Branding is very simple, but if used correctly it can have a huge impact on your business. Branding consists of your name, your logo, the colours you want to use for advertising, and a tagline.

The first aspect of your brand is your business name. Once you have the name, you have to make sure that name links up with all of the above points. We were called KPC Martial Arts when we first started ... because we were a martial arts gym. As we became more and more focused on reality-based self-defense, we re-branded ourselves as KPC Self Defense. KPC Self Defense was an excellent transition, and helped us attract our chosen demographic. Having the name of your school line up with what you're trying to achieve is by far one of the greatest things you can do.

I cannot stress enough how important it is that your name matches your business. You have little hope of attracting the students you want if your name doesn't represent your product. Plus, having to explain over and over again what your business name means gets old really fast.

Too many businesses tend to make their name something very hokey, or way too personal, like a landmark and an animal or energy source, "Master Randy's Chi Centre for Combat Arts". A name like that is way too esoteric, especially in North America. I'm sure that stuff works in other places, but the people you're going to attract with a name like that are going to be all over the place.

Logo ... this one is tough. Everyone's taste is different. My only major advice here is to keep it as simple as possible. The best logos, like the golden arches or the Nike swoosh, are dead simple and very identifiable. You can design your logo yourself, or if you have no idea what to do you can get an artist to do one for you, but for God's sake pay this person! Don't just say it's "for exposure" - artists are so sick of hearing that. If you want multiple versions, and you don't want to pay for a lot of samples (as that can get pricey when you actually pay your artist), there are multiple websites now like 99designs[5] where you can pay a small fee and have dozens of artists pitch you ideas.

Next up is colours. Picking the colours for your advertising and all future branding is difficult. There has been a lot of research done into how colours make people feel. For example, have you ever wondered why almost every fast food brand uses a red and yellow colour scheme? (You guessed it, these colours make you feel hungry.)

A tagline is just another glimpse into your message. For us, it's "KPC Self Defense - Every day you leave a little bit safer." Our old tagline, when we were still a martial arts gym, was "from knife fight to knockout". The tagline is a way to quickly provide a touch more detail about what you do.

---

[5] https://99designs.ca/

Worksheet 2 - Getting Started

What is my message?

What is my specific target demographic?

What is/are my major medium/media?

Potential names:

Logo designers:

Colours:

Tag Line:

5 RED TAPE

All right - at this point you have a great name and you know what you want to accomplish. Now comes the boring and very tedious but needed-to-stay-out-of-jail part ... all the freaking red tape.

In this chapter we will cover a lot of little things you need to do when starting up your business. It's the checklist of things you should do or have before you open your doors.

The first is deciding how you are going to run your business. This will depend on what the options are for running a business in your area. Here in Alberta, the major choices are to either operate as a sole proprietor or to become a corporation. Both of these have great benefits, and we have been both at different times. You need to research which will be best for you.

A business license will be next. Look for a business license in your region, whether it be a city, a rural area, or whatever. Usually these are done by the municipality, so the city/village/town is going to be who issues your business license. It's very important that you have a business license. It helps for any chamber of commerce dealings, and it is usually required when you are setting up wholesale contracts.

Make sure your business name is not taken, and then register it as quickly as possible. Most people weirdly forget this step, but you need to register your business name, and in order to do that you need to do a search to see if anyone else is using that name. You don't want to end up with a WWF to WWE situation, especially early on in your business when you are trying to build name recognition.

Next up, you're going to need insurance. My lawyer is a friend of mine. On his first day in his contracts class, the very first thing they learned was that nobody plans on getting divorced. The same applies to falling out with students. Hopefully in your entire career you never get sued! That hopefulness, however, is about as effective as typing thoughts and prayers on Facebook, which is to say, not at all! You need something a little more tangible, because you never know how people will react.

The type of insurance you will require depends on the specifics of your situation, but get it! Insurance can be a high overhead cost, so you need to build that into your plan of how much your bills are going to be. As well as potentially keeping you out of court, having insurance makes you look much more professional to potential customers. Also, if you're looking for a location, a lot of places won't lease to you unless you have an insurance certificate.

You should also get a lawyer. Seriously. They are a great investment and they can explain all of this stuff to you in a couple of seconds. Attached to that, you're going to need some kind of waiver. Getting a lawyer to write the waiver for you is a one-time fee.

Checklist - Red Tape

- ☐ figure out how to run a business legally
- ☐ register business name
- ☐ business licence
- ☐ insurance
- ☐ get a lawyer

6 BUDGETING

Time for the boring stuff (at least to me). Budgeting may be tedious, but it is important; you need a budget to keep you on track. This area is one of my weak points, so you can learn from my mistakes. Figure this stuff out ahead of time so you don't end up with bills you don't know how to pay because you went a little crazy at the supply store.

You're going to need to go over all your bills and sort out the minimum amount you will need to make. Figure out what the lowest end is, so that you know how you will build your program, and how you will price yourself, and so on (more on this in the following chapters). You'll want to know what you absolutely <u>need</u> to make, and then you also want to plan for the possibility that you're going to blow up at any second. This may sound like new-age-positive-thinking-visualization stuff, but it is just the truth. You never know when your business is going to blow up, and if you only get one chance for success, you don't want to be hesitating and miss the bus.

Too many people get lost in the details of "this is how much money I need to make". They focus on that amount of money; it stays in their head, and they don't move past that amount, so they're always scraping to make sure all of their bills are paid and then they're stuck in this paycheque-to-paycheque world. I'm not saying that just having a plan to become big is going to prevent that; there have been times when we've been paycheque-to-paycheque in our business, but we've always come through because we had a grand scheme of how to make more money.

I want you to build an infrastructure where you're definitely going to be making at least the minimum amount you need, so you're not freaking out and borrowing money off your parents, but I also want you to have a system in place where you can blow up when the opportunity arises. Knowing what your top end is, can be just as important as knowing what your bottom end is. For example with KPC, in my brick-and-mortar business, we are limited as to how many students we can accommodate. We can only hold a maximum of a hundred and twenty students; and that's a hundred and twenty students over four classes, thirty per class. With private lessons, we can probably only accommodate about forty people there. So our top end is about one hundred and sixty students on the books. We should always be reaching for that one hundred and sixty. We should not be focusing on our minimum requirements for the business. That being said, you still should know that you need a certain number of students, this many private lessons, this many seminars, this many t-shirt sales, this many group classes. Whatever your dynamic is, you should know what the low end is, but don't focus on it. Focus on shooting for the high end. If you're always shooting for the stars, you can at least land on the moon. Make sure that when you're doing that, you're shooting for something incredible.

Once you have established your bottom and top ends, I want you to set up a yearly operating budget for things that you will be paying for constantly. This will help keep you honest, especially during those times when you are flush with cash.

Each business is a little different, but every business needs a marketing budget. How much money are you going to spend getting the word out? When you start out, your marketing budget will be small, as you won't have a lot of capital to work with. As you grow, though, so should your budget - it has to. Staying within a budget gives you, as a business owner, two great benefits. First, it teaches discipline. (It is really hard for some of us - especially outgoing salespeople - to stick within a budget when times are good!) Second, it forces you to become more creative, instead of just throwing money at problems. A lot of things that people pay for out of habit can be worked around. Do you NEED new bags, or is black duct tape fine for a bit? Keeping within a budget will force you to look for other options, and sometimes those options turn out to be far better.

Set up budgets for any recurring expense; office supplies, marketing, gas, equipment replacement, etc. Only you will know what expenses keep coming up. Create the budget and <u>stick to it</u>. When the time is right and you hit a new threshold in your business, you will be able to increase the items in the budget. I have seen far too many people go crazy and get burned early on in the business buying stuff that they didn't need.

7 GOALS

If it can't be measured, it can't be improved. Setting goals is a very basic part of any business plan. Unfortunately, most people don't bother thinking about this.

After you have your budget all figured out, you will need to set goals so that you know what you are working towards. Only then can you make a plan to get there. Once your plan is in place, you will need to track it, track it, and keep on tracking it! There is no point in setting goals if you have no way of tracking or measuring whether or not you are meeting them.

The first thing you will need to figure out is what parameters you are working with. Each business is going to be very different, so figure these out based on your business and what medium you are using. If you have zero idea where to start, take a look at my basic goals as a template. For my business as it stands, I need to track memberships sold, private lessons sold, and lastly, shirts sold. These are all the variable income factors relied on by my gym. Like we said in the budgeting chapter, you need to know your minimum numbers in order to survive.

I want you to create a realistic maximum for each area. As I said, for us, memberships are one hundred and twenty at maximum, private lessons are maximum of twenty hours a week, and as for the t-shirts ... well, there is no limit! I want to sell all the t-shirts!

Once you have a min/max projection, it's time to make a plan to reach those numbers!

If you have been to an interview you have inevitably heard the question "Where do you want to be in five years? What's your five-year plan?" As annoying as this question is, a five-year plan is a fantastic idea for your business. You need a five-year plan to start out with, and then build your subsequent plans around that. When I first opened KPC in 2009 as a full-time location (we started part-time in 2005) the first thing I did was make a five-year plan. Again, if it can't be tracked, it can't be measured, and if it can't be measured, it can't be fixed. When we opened the gym I made a five-year goal sheet, including how many students I wanted to have, and how much money I needed to make. It was a great way to see where I needed to direct my efforts.

Having a plan is good, but don't have it set in stone. Every plan fails at first contact. What I mean here by "fail" is that you might surpass your goals very quickly. We blew our first five-year plan out of the water in under two years. I had set the bar very low on all my metrics, including my exit strategy for my day job. So, I sat back down and made a new plan, and went full-time at my dream, in what (to me) seemed like record time. I still worked a part-time job for six months after that, but it became my second priority. The day I went full-time at my dream was one of the best days of my life, and it will probably be the same for you.

So, how do you write up a five-year plan? It's simple! Go to the worksheet at the back of this chapter (or take out a piece of paper) and write "in five years" on the top of it. Then, think about your goals. Whether you will shoot for the stars or stay conservative, figure out what you think five years of working at this will look like. The plan shouldn't just include the business side of things. Where do you want to be in your relationships? Where you want to be in your personal life? All of this is relevant. Remember that you are doing this so you can live a life you love ... so that life needs to be part of your plan. The plan should also include all of your financial goals. Do you want to own a house, a car, a motorcycle? Do you want to have the ability to go on a trip once a year or pay off that cursed debt? Once you have set your goals, they will inform your business plan. Where you want your business to be is going to be the main factor in all of this.

Once your goals are set, you will need to make an actual concrete plan for how to get there. If your five-year plan is that you want to be making a hundred thousand dollars a year at the business, and you're making a hundred thousand dollars a year in a year and a half, or two years, way to crush it! Time to readjust your plan! But if in five years, you're only making eighty thousand dollars, you can then go back to the plan and say "okay, where did I go wrong?" You might even look back and find out that you didn't go wrong at all. Remember, money is good ... but so is having your kids know what you look like, or not having your partner leave. I firmly believe that your business should facilitate your life, and not the other way around.

Now that you have your five-year plan, you need a metric to measure your success with the plan. We're going to use money as an example here, but you can choose any metric you want. Let's say your financial goals are that you need the business to make at least X dollars a year, and you want the business to be making Y dollars a year. Both the X and the Y values will change as your business grows. The bottom end you started with will change as your goals do. You need to make X dollars a year, so how are you going to accomplish that through those five years? You should know that eight out of ten businesses fail within the first eighteen months - those people most likely did not have a plan.

After you set your five-year goals, start making subsequent smaller plans and goals to bring that to fruition. What do I mean by that? If, in five years, you plan to have a hundred students, how many clients do you need to gain and retain per month/session/year, in order to reach that five-year goal?

Look at the numbers you set, and then build a strategy. This is what we are working on here at KPC now ... we never used the metrics like this before. I had a five-year plan when it was just me, but now that we have multiple employees and are looking at opening another location, we have to have those worksheets that everybody hates in the sales field, dictating what we need to accomplish every month.

You need to know your business inside and out! You need to know how many clients you have to have in order to pay the bills, and you need to know how many clients you have to retain in order to grow the business. You need to know how many clients you generally lose per session. The average business loses ten to twenty-five percent of its clients each year. These kinds of statistics are great to know, but they are not canon. Take this as a personal challenge, not an excuse to be average. The stats say you will lose ten percent of your clients a year - so figure out how to only lose eight percent! You need to be above and beyond all the averages if you don't want to end up on the same side as the eighty percent of businesses that fail.

Next, we need the steps to get you there. You are going to repeat the steps you used in creating your five-year goals, and make a goal set for three years, one year, six months, three months. You can go as small as you want, even down to daily goals. The more data you collect, the better you can analyze your business. Once your goals are in place, formulate your plans for how to get there. (We will get into that in the second part of this book.)

Running a business without a plan is by far the most chaotic, hectic thing you can do. Personally, I love the mayhem of it, because there's always something different going on, but it isn't the best way of doing things. A plan will protect you, it will be your armour against the chaos of running a business and will help you prioritize your time. Honestly, everything seems important when you are super busy. You need to understand every one of your metrics. Each one of those areas where you generate income or grow your business needs to be checked. You need to make a metric that works, and you need to be regularly checking where you're at. If you are above on your metric, that's fantastic - how did you get above it? If you're *way* above it, then you should definitely readjust all your plans in the future! Every time you hit another goal, you're going to readjust. Every six months to a year, you're going to be reevaluating.

The last thing I want to say on plans and goals is that I want you to have an exit strategy. I know this is counterintuitive for most business books, but not every single person that reads this book is going to succeed in their first business. There's so many stories out there - "Michael Jordan was kicked off of his high school basketball team" and "it took Bill Gates eight hundred loans to get started". The simple fact is that you might not succeed on your first try.

KPC is the third version of what I was doing. I very rarely meet a person who still has the original version of their business going. Why am I mentioning this? I am not trying to dishearten you - I want you to keep going, keep working, keep trying on your business. The reality is, though, that sometimes the business is not going to work, so I want you to have an exit strategy. My first business was a business called "Dojo on the Go". It was me and my Ford Ranger, a punching bag and some pads, and I would go to your house and personally teach you martial arts. I would come to you, I would train you on my own gear, and I charged very little. It was unrealistic. The profit was too low, and I hadn't accounted for things like overhead … and taxes. Did I quit? Hell yes I quit, but then I went right back to the drawing board. You need to have a line in the sand where you will concede that "this is not working". If you do not make a certain amount of money, or if you have not left your day job in a certain amount of time, I need you to stop the business you're doing, re-evaluate, adjust and then get moving again. Please don't end up becoming one of those people on *Dragon's Den* (or *Shark Tank* for you Yanks) who are on their third mortgage still trying to fund their board game.

Worksheet 3 - Goals

Five year life goals

Five year business goals

Three year business goals

One year

Three months

Monthly

8 PRICING YOURSELF

One of the hardest things to do in any business is to decide how much you should charge for your services. I think most people just take a shot in the dark, or maybe do some market research, or just arbitrarily charge a number they think is fair to them. In this chapter I'd like to explain to you a couple of different methods for pricing yourself, as well as how to not to price yourself out of business.

One of the biggest mistakes most entrepreneurs make is pricing their service far too low. They are just so happy to be doing what they love, that they don't want to "overcharge" or seem "greedy". This is especially prevalent in martial arts, so much so that I did a rant on it, titled "You Get What You Pay For"[6]. Most people who love what they do just want to get their services out there, in order to help people out. This is especially true in the training world. You just want to make your clients healthier, or help them lose weight, or feel better in their clothes, or make them safer. You don't want them freaking out when they have to run to the grocery store at night because of the unseen boogeyman outside. This passion that got you into your business might be the one thing that kills it. I have met so many passionate people in client-based services that

---

[6] https://www.youtube.com/watch?v=qmGltxpOgBc

underprice themselves so much that they run themselves out of business. They might need to take second jobs, or it just becomes too stressful to keep going.

Every single one of you out there reading this book has some kind of skill set you want to push, whether it be personal training, self-defense, presentations, or anything else. There is some service or skill set that you have, that you want other people to have. The issue with this is that if you're doing something that's never been done before, it can be really hard to find a price point. There are a few methods I suggest when finding the right price for your business.

Straight up - if you can't get paid, then you're going to be extremely stressed, and if you're extremely stressed, you won't be able to give everything you have to the business. Making enough money and paying your bills and overhead are the hardest parts of starting a business. If you never manage to get to the point where that is taken care of, you will never reach the next level of your business, which is expansion. It's hard to see the forest when you spend all your energy focusing on the trees.

When we first started with our pricing, we were pulling numbers out of the air. We said, "classes are worth this much money, and with this much money we can make about this much per year, and that's what we need to run". We totally failed to take into account all of the infrastructure crap that needed to be paid for, like a business license, advertising, the website, taxes and savings. This was a major error for us. Now it is time for you to learn from my mistakes!

Model One: Overhead Model (for new businesses)
When assigning pricing with the overhead model, you start by taking all of your costs to actually operate the business. You then take what you need to make as a salary, and add in that along with all those other costs - don't forget that you will be putting away about thirty percent of your income for taxes and savings, so the numbers you work from should be after-tax numbers, or *net* rather than *gross*. You divide that total by the number of services you charge for, and that gives you your standard price per service.

(This would change if your services are not all of equal value.) For example, a lot of people run monthly programs. If your entire income is based on these monthly classes, and you have a certain number of students on average taking classes per month, you divide your total monthly overhead by that number of students. Let's say you needed to be making fifty-four dollars a month per person; you would divide that fifty-four dollars by seventy percent (to account for the taxes) and find that you need to charge about eighty dollars per month per client in order to break even.

This is where we adjust - if the number you come out with is way out of line with your goals, you will need to adjust the base price. Make sure that these prices line up with the goals you established. This is by far the best way to set up a new business.

Sale pricing is an area where a lot of people get into trouble with their pricing. They set their standard price at the bare minimum they need to survive, and then when they put things on sale they shoot themselves in the foot. If you plan to be running sales on occasion, you must make sure your base price has some wiggle room, and never, ever - unless you are going out of business - reduce your price to a level at or below your base. If you need to make twenty-five dollars a session in order to keep the lights on, don't do a sale for twenty-five dollars. Instant cash flow seems like a good idea, but it always ends up costing you in the end. In this respect, you need to treat yourself like a product. You would never sell a house for less than you paid for it, unless you absolutely had to. The same holds true for your business.

Model Two: Market Research (for new or existing businesses)
When you're setting pricing, another good approach is to do it through market research. Market research is usually just called "doing your homework" - you should be doing this in any standard business plan anyways. Do your homework, call all of the places around you that are doing something similar to you. We are talking about client-based services, so personal training, martial arts, nutritionists, anything relevant to what you offer. Call around, talk to personal trainers, talk to fitness gyms, talk to other martial arts gyms, talk to other self-defense gyms, talk to anybody in that

field, and see what they're charging. Take all those numbers, find an average, and decide whether you want to go with an undercut model (which I don't suggest) or an overprice model. Both models do work to some extent, but there are pros and cons to each of them.

I'm going to advise against the undercut model. I know it sounds crazy, because we all "know" that the lowest price is the "best" price ... but that is not true when it comes to client-based services. That thought process comes from product-based services; if I can get a car for five thousand dollars, or I can get the same car elsewhere for three thousand dollars, I'm going to buy the car for three thousand dollars. When it comes to client-based services, however, most people would prefer to work with the best. Two things will be going through their minds while they're evaluating your service; the amount of money they can spend on the service, and getting the most value for that money.

For example, in our gym, my partner and I have different pricing for private lessons. He charges private lessons at a slightly lower rate than I do, and he often has more clients. However, the customers he gets sometimes have problems paying; they ask for extensions, they need credit, etc., because those clients were typically buying based on the price, not on the service. Usually when price is the deciding factor, it's because of financial circumstances. This is not true of all of Thor's clients, just the ones who chose him based on price. They're good clients, as long as you're willing to work with them and give extensions as needed, but they're not great for bill payments. On the other hand, my clients, who are paying a little bit more even though there's a cheaper service available, are much more reliable payers. They opted for the more expensive coach, because they wanted the "best person for the job". People with that type of thinking, who want to train with "the best", are usually willing to pay whatever the price is to train with that person, especially in North America.

You may be tempted to price really high now, as it may be starting to sound like the better option - but you must remember that clients who don't worry about money are far rarer than the ones who shop for price. (There is a reason Walmart is so successful.)

There's two ways to run your business, the "over" or the "under". My favourite way of explaining this is with the "Lincoln and Ford" model. Generally speaking, everybody understands that a Lincoln is a high-end car, and Fords are considered to be lower-end cars. (There are lots of memes about how Fords are crappy ... even though I drive a Ford myself, and I love it!) A high-end Ford and a low-end Lincoln are almost identical, minus some branding and a couple of aesthetic changes. Why, then, is the high-end Ford still ten thousand dollars cheaper than the low-end Lincoln, when they are both produced by the same company? The reason is that some people want that luxury. There's a reason why Kia hasn't taken over the world in car sales. People are still going to want Porsches - being able to afford a Porsche is a status symbol.

Your pricing model should include both a Ford model and a Lincoln model. For us, the Ford model is our group classes. Group classes are very inexpensive, so they're accessible to almost everyone. They are a great way to go. We get more people in, who we can potentially upsell later. We also have the Lincoln model, which is our private lessons. Private lessons offer a higher level of training, because in an hour of one-on-one training, you can accomplish much more than you can accomplish in an hour of group classes. Clients who want better, tailored training, and better scheduling, can access that by paying a higher rate.

Having both options has been super effective for us, but you can go either way. You can have both low-end and high-end options, or you can go with just low-end, or just high-end. Don't forget about the "dentist problem" though, like I mentioned before. There are only so many hours in a day, and you are just as bound by those hours as anyone else. If you're doing private lessons at twenty-five dollars an hour, and I'm doing them at seventy-five dollars an hour, then yeah, you might be busier than me, because you have six customers a day. In two hours, though, I can make as much money as you made in six. Be very aware of what your time is worth, and be willing to price yourself higher the more successful you become.

Your market research will show you whether the prices you came up with make sense for your area, or if you are just out to lunch.

Model Three: Proven Price Point (existing, long-term businesses)
The last way to do pricing is something called your "proven price point". This is the advice I gave to Rory Miller, and it is the advice I give to anyone who has been doing this for a while.

Proven price point is simple. It is just the amount of money you have historically been making while doing what you do. When you start off, this will be all over the map. You may make a hundred dollars one time, and four hundred and fifty dollars another. The best way to know how much you can charge is by looking at your history. With that knowledge, you can set prices that you already know people are willing to pay ... because they already have paid that much. I went through this example with Rory who is now charging himself out at four thousand dollars a weekend. (He started off at twelve hundred dollars, went to two thousand, twenty-five hundred, then he jumped to four thousand dollars as his fame rose.) He was plotting to build a new program for somebody, and as we were trying to price it out, we went to the "proven price point" - how much is his time worth? He has a proven price point of two hundred and fifty dollars an hour. He's charging four grand for a sixteen hour seminar, or two hundred and fifty dollars per hour, and people are paying that - it's his proven price point. So, when we were building his next project, we billed it out at two hundred and fifty dollars an hour. Knowing what you are worth is super important.

This is especially relevant when you're starting a seminar tour, if that is in your wheelhouse. That is what I am working on the most right now; doing a bunch of experiments with different ways to run seminars. Deciding how to charge for that is hard; you don't want to charge too little, because you don't want potential clients to think you're cheap or that you're not going to make enough money, and you also don't want to charge too much, because then you end up scared that you're going to lose the sale.

I challenge you right now to take your average income from whatever you've done, such as seminars, or workshops, or whatever. Take your average price for a day, divide it by the number of hours you put into it in a day, and that number is your proven price point if you have an existing business. If you don't have an existing business established already, then market research becomes key. It is amazing the difference price makes in sales, and it's also amazing the difference it makes in promotions. My favourite example of this is in raising prices, because a lot of people are scared to raise prices for their students. Even if you do lose students, you're probably going to lose the students who were the most problematic anyway. If you subscribe to the "eighty/twenty rule", it's reasonable to say that eighty percent of your problems probably come from twenty percent of your clients. If you raise your prices, it's pretty much guaranteed that you'll lose that twenty percent of your clients (which sucks and sounds scary) but you'll replace them with better clients, who are not as much maintenance. You'll be doing less work, and making more money.

The first time we ever raised our private lesson price was probably in 2012. When we were mobile, I was teaching private lessons at twenty-five dollars an hour. Then, once we moved into a physical location, doing twenty-five dollars an hour wasn't feasible anymore. We raised the price to forty dollars an hour, and we stayed at forty dollars an hour for about three years. The hourly income was decent, we were booking three or four a day, plus we did classes on top, so I was making an okay living - but I wasn't killing it. As our costs went up, with rent increasing on my space, taxes going up, and having to advertise more as we grew, our prices were not reflecting that. We had to raise prices; there was no way around it.

I decided to raise my prices from forty dollars an hour to fifty dollars an hour, so that our average ten-pack was five hundred dollars for ten private lessons. Nothing changed, everybody still paid, it was no big deal, but then - a funny thing happened. A gym in the area went out of business, and they were selling all their equipment, and I wanted it! We didn't have a lot of money in reserve, so I decided, "hey, let's put privates on sale, tell people what it's for, and we'll see what happens". We put our private lessons price back down to forty dollars an hour for one weekend. During that sale, we sold one hundred and thirty hours of private lessons, for no other reason than because it was a "sale". People would rather pay more all the time and then find a deal, than pay consistently low prices. There were people who had no idea we were forty dollars an hour before, because they were like, "oh, private lessons, whatever". Then we went to fifty dollars an hour, and nothing changed, my business stayed the same except we were making more money. Put the privates on sale, and all of a sudden, BOOM, we sold way more than we've ever sold before, and easily made enough money to buy all the equipment.

Make sure that when you're pricing yourself, you're still pricing yourself to the point where you can make money, where you can live, pay all your bills, and put some money into savings. I talked about this earlier, but I'll hammer it again, *thirty percent.* You want to be putting *thirty percent* away for taxes, for incidentals, for whatever. When you build your price point, don't just build it the way I did the first time, which was "I need to make this much money to pay my bills, so I'll divide it and not include taxes and upkeep and overhead". You might not think you have a lot of overhead and upkeep, but cleaning supplies cost money, whiteboard markers cost money, toilet paper costs money. Equipment costs money! So many things can happen. Your gear could break, your chains could bust, the mats get dirty and ripped, somebody gets hurt, somebody breaks something, you need safety equipment, etc. There are always going to be those incidentals, and you want to have that money in reserve to cover them.

Remember that prices will always be changing. As the world and your business move forward, so you will your rates. Pay attention, and when you do have to raise prices, make sure there is a solid reason so that when your clients ask you why, you can give them an honest answer.

Worksheet 4 - Pricing via the Overhead Model

Lease:

Insurance:

Salary:

Other: utilities, advertising, etc.

Total divided by net price per service = base cost per client

PART TWO

MARKETING AND SALES

9 OVERVIEW

Let's be honest - this part is why most of you bought this book. You all want a little piece of the Randy King action!

Honestly, who can blame you?

Why the hell does a 36-year-old chubby Canadian have so many fans? How does he run such a big school, and get to travel to teach so much?

The reason is *marketing*. I am probably one of the best out there at marketing, and now it is time to pass along some of my mojo.

Marketing and sales are way easier than most people think. If you listen to people who do marketing for a living, it's easy to believe that it's an esoteric art form. It is in their interest to make it seem WAY harder than it is, so that you will pay them to do it for you. Why do I know this? Well, it was my job for years to do just that. But like the masked magician said (you may have to Google that if you are under 30 … or if you actually dated in the 90's) it is time to reveal these mysteries …

(Man, I wish I could include dramatic music in a book …)

Basically, you need to know two things. The first is that no matter how big technology gets or how fancy the analytics are, most people just want to work with businesses that fit their needs, and with people they trust. The evolution of marketing tools (e.g. the Internet) is all about finding new ways to earn that trust. The second is the notion that sales is just enthusiasm transferred. If you are pumped about what you do, the client will be as well. The way to accomplish these two goals has changed pretty dramatically as the Internet has evolved into the social web we deal with now. Different tools, but the goal remains the same.

There are entire shelves in bookstores dedicated to the arts of marketing and sales. In this part of the book I will sum up what you need to know.

The most common marketing and sales term in the world is the "sales funnel", pictured[7] below. (I am sure some of you are rolling your eyes at this ... not another sales funnel explanation! Well, too bad! Not everything is about you.

The New Marketing and Sales Funnel

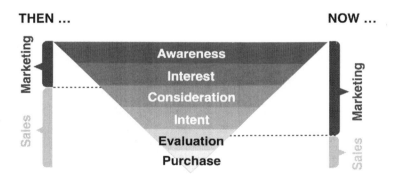

A sales funnel is a great way to explain the process of turning leads into clients. Looking at a basic sales funnel, starting at the top you have just general *awareness* of the fact that your business exists. The day people started to go from "what is KPC?" to "oh, I think I have heard of you, you do stick fighting, right?" was a fantastic day! This level of the funnel includes all of your

---

[7] Adapted from https://stevepatrizidotcom.files.wordpress.com/2012/10/newmarketingsalesfunnel1.jpg

marketing; traditional, online, referrals, word-of-mouth, signs ... all of it.

The next level down, we have *interest*. These are the people that know about you, and may want to do something like you do. This group is smaller than just those people who know you exist. My Grandma is a huge fan, but does not care to partake in a knife defense workshop. Interest is driven by marketing as well. In fact, in the new age of business, marketing plays a larger role than ever, as social media gives us more time to make arguably better choices by providing more info and building more trust.

The next level is *consideration*. These are the people that are actually deciding between you and a few other service providers. You may have some contact with them ... and fifteen years ago you would have at least received a phone call. In today's generation, this is the phase where you want your social media marketing and website to be on point.

Next is *intent*. This is where you get prospective clients to try a free class or come by and have a chat. You want to get them trying out the service. We are not selling them yet, just letting them come in and try a class. I am against paid trials. They make sense, but that pay-to-play mentality for trying out services doesn't really fly anymore.

This is followed by the *evaluation* phase, where people are deciding whether to buy. This is the stage where the actual sales kick in. On the diagram this seems like a small part, and it's true that the group here is very small, but here is where you need to transfer that enthusiasm, ask for the sale and follow up, so that finally we hit the *purchase* level.

In this part of the book we will be exploring all of these levels in more detail, as well as teaching you about the ever-scary social media, and how to create great content to get your name out there and to keep people engaged. In each section, I will go over the things I feel will give the best bang for your buck. You already know what you want to be, now let's get you there!

One more thing - just like everything in your business, you need to track your marketing. There will be plenty of tips here on how to do that, but always, always keep track! It is important to see what is working and what is not. You want to able to track the numbers on what you are doing so that you will know where to cut from and where to double down.

10 TRADITIONAL MARKETING
(Awareness: Funnel Level 1)

The top level of the funnel is awareness - this is a pretty big chunk of information as it involves a whole mess of things. I am going to break it down into three parts: traditional marketing and network marketing in this chapter, and internet marketing in the next chapter. At this stage of your "funnel", it is just about getting your name out there as much as possible. People first need to know that you are around, before they can even think about buying from you.

Traditional marketing:
This type of lead generation is actually going the way of the dodo, as social media marketing is becoming an unstoppable juggernaut. Traditional marketing costs money, is very hard to measure, and it takes some work. That being said, people do still expect to see the old-school methods, so if you can use them cheaply enough they will lend credibility to your business.

By traditional marketing, I mean pretty much anything that is not done online. The encompasses a huge - and I mean huge - number of touch points, from billboards to radio to sign spinners. I am going to boil down just the ones that are best for startups and small businesses; the ones I have used. Right off the bat, you are going to want to get some business cards made up.

I know, I know, why did I let my grandfather write this part of the book?

Honestly though, business cards are still a great way to demonstrate that you are a professional. The thing with cards is people don't actually take them anymore; they usually just snap a pic with their phone. So yes, you will need business cards … but don't order too many, as you won't be going through as many as you think. Apps like WorldCard Mobile are a fantastic way to organize the business cards you receive as well. When you get your cards printed, keep it simple: name, title, and relevant stuff, website and contact info. Don't go crazy. Make sure your logo is on it. Lastly, maybe add an offer on it, like one free class or 10% off. This way the card has an actual value as well, it is not just trash.

The next traditional marketing option for startups is posters. We still use posters at KPC, sadly it is hard to tell how useful they are. Posters are a cheap way of getting your name out there. In order to make a great poster, keep it simple. Include all of your business card info, as well as maybe something on those five things that make your business stand out. Once again, you won't need a lot of these. They stay up for a while after you've found places to put them up. If you want to track your poster campaign, I recommend either putting up an offer different from the one on your business card, so you know where it came from, or using different contact names on the poster. Maybe use just your first name or a nickname so that when you get that email or that phone call, you know the lead came from the posters specifically. Remember: track as much as you can!

Lastly, get some signage, whether you have windows, or a storefront, or even a sandwich board for when you are doing something in the area. The more places people see your stuff, the more you will stay "top of mind". That way, when they are ready to buy, they will think of you first. There is a correlation between Coke being both the number one soft drink in the world and the company that spends the most on advertising. People rarely say offhand "Grab me a Pepsi".

Aside from business cards, posters, and signage, some information pamphlets are a decent idea, but not essential. Those will be used more as a takeaway, and less as a way to bring people in. They will be used during marketing events, not as lead generators.

Network marketing:
No one is an island, and neither is any business. The more people you get talking about your service, the better. I know this is a no-brainer, but seriously, you need to get in front of as many people as possible! First off, open houses and demonstrations are by far the best way to start doing this type of marketing. If you can, and especially at the beginning, give your services away for free - or for as little as possible. We are starting to do free "lunch and learns" at local businesses to get the word out. These are great ways to start building clients, referrals, and reviews.

Reviews are VERY important in this day and age. Remember, it is all about building trust. We live in an age where everything is reviewed, and people take it really seriously. The more people you have saying that you are awesome, the better your business will do. Also - I can't believe I have to say this, but I see it all the time - DON'T REVIEW YOURSELF! You laugh, but man is it prevalent.

There is an old-school marketing statistic, that says if someone has an exceptional time they will tell two people about it, and if they have an average time they will say nothing, but if they have a bad time they will tell at least seven people about it. Kind of sucks right? Well, too bad, that is the world we live in. People would much rather complain than compliment; this is the norm. People who like your service won't be gushing about it as much as you think they might (or as much as you want them to). So, after you provide your service, you will need to first ask them for reviews of your business (or even letters of recommendation for services well done), and then give them an incentive to tell everyone. There is a reason why referral rewards are so popular - they work!

A lot of the time, people seem to be against incentivizing good recommendations, feeling that the work should speak for itself, so why lose money on a customer that they would have gotten anyway? That kind of thinking is just stupid. Referral incentives are the best way to ask for referrals without seeming like you are begging. You are literally doing your customers a favour. I remind my students <u>constantly</u> about my referral rewards, to keep it fresh in their minds that we need people, and they can save money by bringing people to us.

Make sure your referral rewards don't price you down below what you need to make per client though - never discount past your minimum. You don't want to get yourself in financial trouble helping your clients out.

11 INTERNET MARKETING AND SEARCH ENGINE OPTIMIZATION (SEO)
(Awareness: Funnel Level 1 continued)

Internet marketing is kind of a new thing. A lot of people don't understand it, a lot of people believe they understand it, and a lot more people try and charge you tons of money because they believe they understand it the best. In reality, it's a learning curve, all the time, for everybody. This is true, so much so that people will try and blind you with jargon. First, let's get you up to speed on all that internet mumbo-jumbo. Then, let's help you to understand what you need, what you don't need, and where you should be investing your money when it comes to websites, email marketing and SEO.

Depending on your age, you're going to have a different perception of the Internet. Some of you may have no understanding, and think it's pointless, and some of you might believe it is one of the best things in the world. Some of you may have more knowledge than I do ... if that is the case, shoot me a message, my contact info is at the end of this book. If you have any other tips or tricks or things that worked for you, tell us and we can share it! My follow-up plan for after the release of this book is to have a page for business strategies, that way everyone can keep up-to-date on all of the things that are happening in the business world, which is always evolving.

How will people find out about you on the Internet? It's simple - they will type in keywords on a search engine, most likely Google[8], and your website might just pop up. This can happen without any effort on your part, just like when people saw a poster back in 1991. They could just happen to come across your business.

How can you *make sure* that more people come across you in this manner? Let's talk about the monster that is Google, and dab our feet in the pool of search engine optimization (SEO). If you don't know what Google is, we're in a lot of trouble. In short, Google is the largest search engine in the world. It is the most popular by far, and a multi-billion dollar company. I'm sure you have used it; and if not, I'm sure your children have used it. If for some reason you're reading this as an e-book in a cave somewhere, on a Kindle you stole from a hiker, you definitely need to get to know what Google is.

Google uses an algorithm that goes through websites constantly and determines whether a website is popular, current and still active. This is the essence of SEO - learning how to take better advantage of the algorithm, which we will get into a little later. First, how do you demonstrate that your website is current? The easiest way is by updating it. You want to update your website every couple of weeks ideally, every three months at the latest. That's one of my sins, we definitely don't update our website enough. Luckily that's getting rectified, not by me because that's one of my weaknesses, but by a member of my team. Updating the site is an easy way to keep you relevant on the web, and the best way to keep it up-to-date is to create content!

Another little-known fact is that most search engines now give higher priority to websites that are mobile-ready. This seems to be the thing I've been harping on the most with people that I'm consulting with - Google now gives more juice to websites with a mobile version. Mobile searches are very quickly overtaking the

---

[8] www.google.com

world, with sixty-five percent of searches for businesses done on mobile as of the moment I wrote this, and I guarantee it is even higher now. If your website is just a static page with no mobile version, you're already going to be dropped lower on Google's search engine, and that's going to make you the third, fourth, fifth, tenth choice when people are looking for businesses that do what you do. If you have not caught on yet, you want to be as high up on the search engine results as possible.

This is where search engine optimization comes in. This is probably the next most important battle, because you can have the prettiest website in the world, a fully functioning website with the best sales generator - but if nobody's visiting the page, it's useless. The Internet has a symbiotic relationship between search engines, websites and destinations, content, and social media. If all of those things aren't firing on all cylinders, you're going to have a weak Internet presence, and that could be disastrous.

Let's get more into search engine optimization. Some consider it the snake oil of our generation; people don't really get what SEO is, they either think they don't need it at all, or at the other end of the spectrum they put too much money into it. Very simply, what search engine optimization does is game the matrix. It makes sure that when people are searching for services like yours, they find you first. Being "first" means being the top pick that comes out of the search. How do you become the top choice? By using keywords and Internet tricks. (I use Google as an example here, but saying Google is like saying Kleenex when I mean tissue ... the same tactics will work on any search engine out there.) You want to make sure that you are as high up on those search engine results as possible.

So, how do you get search engine optimization? And why do companies charge so much money to do it for you? This is where a lot of people get confused.

There are two ways of selling something. There's *over-educating* people, and then there's *consultative selling*.

Over-educating people is the method of throwing lots of fancy words and terms at the client. This is to show them how much the sales person knows, to show that they're an expert, so that the client says, "you know what, this is too much information for me, I'm never going to be able to handle this, so you just take over."

Consultative selling involves looking at the needs of the person and helping them with what they need. When I used to make money in sales, I was a consultative salesperson. I wasn't trying to upsell people, I was trying to determine their needs and find out what that person wanted, and then from that point forward I would get them what they needed, not because it gave me the most commission, but because it fit their needs. That worked out really well for me in my career, and it's worked out since. I still do it to this day when people call me and say "oh, my son is looking to compete in MMA"; I don't say "Awesome, we're like MMA and you can come and train with us". I tell them straight up that our gym doesn't fit their needs, and here is who they can call, but if they're ever looking for a self-defense gym, definitely come back to us.

Most people working in SEO are using the first method, over-education. They're selling a product, and they need as many people as possible using their product or service. So they give you a whole bunch of jargon, facts and figures and percentages, just trying to blow your mind with what's going on.

Simply put, the type of business you're in determines how much search engine optimization you will need. The more you know your message, the less likely that a lot of people will be doing what you do. This means that right out of the gate, you do not need to put that much money into SEO. Plumbers, electricians, salespeople, restaurants ... those people need search engine optimization. When somebody's looking around, usually people are going to choose one of the top three search engine results. They go to Google, and search for "restaurant". The first few that come up, they're definitely going to pick one of those first two or three. Nobody goes to the second page of results to keep looking, unless they're super hipster and trying to impress somebody, or they're a food reviewer or critic. Being in the top three is pretty easy in most service-based fields, and especially if you are true to your message.

Edmonton, has, per capita, the most *tae kwon do* schools in Canada. If you are a *tae kwon do* school in my city, then yeah, search engine optimization is a good idea! Will you need an outside company to do it? That depends ... but I don't think you do. If you keep your website active, if you're constantly producing content and posting it, if you have active social media, and you use back-links, you should not need outside help. Back-links are other websites that link back to you. Google looks at that and applies all of those back-links towards the credibility of your site. The more places you can put your website, the better - I like to add my website to all my emails as part of my signature, on all of my blogs, all of our advertising, everywhere we get a chance to; it all contributes to our credibility. The more places you exist on the Internet, the more seriously the algorithm of the search engines takes you, and it puts you higher up.

If you're in a hyper-competitive area, there are companies that do search engine optimization. I've never used a company like that to date.

Learning what keywords you should use is the cheapest way to get great SEO. For us, "reality-based" and "self-defense" are our major keywords. We want those everywhere, so all of our advertising says it, our logo says it, the blogs say it, the videos say it ... in everything we do, we're saying "reality-based self-defense" or "no-nonsense self-defense", because that's the niche I wanted. When people type "self-defense" into their search engine, we should be popping up first, because ours is the website where that word appears most frequently. This is called "keywording". You can go to Google Adwords and they have a tool for keywording, for your industry, it will give you the most-searched terms. The more places you can put the most-searched-for terms on your website, the better, but you have to make it organic. Don't just go jamming words in, or throwing hashtags around like a teen on spring break, because Google's algorithm can see through that now.

The more places you can use the most searched-for words in your industry, the better. So if you're a personal trainer and your niche is that you want to do fat loss, then the more places you put the terms "fat loss", "weight loss goals", "challenge" - all that kind of stuff - the better, and the higher up your website will appear for clients looking for that sort of thing.

Search engine optimization is very easy to do, through keywords, back-linking, constant updates, having a mobile site, and creating content. Whether you're blogging, doing videos, or whatever, make sure you're constantly updating that content to your website as well as to social media.

Review of free SEO:

- Make your page mobile-friendly
- Use relevant keywords for your business as much as possible
- Update your site frequently
- Add social media badges
- Create content and upload it to your site

12 YOUR WEBSITE
(Interest: Funnel Level 2)

All right, so your potential customers know who you are and are interested in what you provide. Step one is done ... so now what? This stage is where you need someplace to send prospective clients to find more information about what you do and why your business is the best choice!

Many of these points will influence various levels of your sales funnel; social media, for example, is a great way to build trust, but it's also a great way to make people aware of your services. (I would not be surprised if in under five years Facebook outranks Google for searches.) As you read on, bear in mind that the more of these areas that you do well with, the better overall your sales funnel will be as well.

Let's start off with the basics. The most basic thing in the world is your website. Your website is one of the places you don't want to get cheap on. You want your website to be one of the best, if not *the* best, websites in your area. The simple fact of the matter is that your website is usually your first impression. There's no other way that people are going to get to know you as quickly or as functionally. The time of print and posters and Yellow Page ads is pretty much over - in fact, even the Yellow Pages do digital promotion now.

You need to decide who is going to create your website. Many people do their own, or have a friend design it. If you want to outsource, you can hire a web designer, or you can use a service that will build a stock website for you. All of these are great options, just go with whatever fits your budget. Make sure, though, that your website is nice, up-to-date and uncluttered! The major purpose of a website is to provide information and draw in sales. All of your future marketing will be bringing people back to your website, so really invest whatever you are able into it. Your website will become the hub of both your online and offline marketing, it is the place where you will be constantly sending people ... so make sure that it's well-done.

Here are a couple of tips on what you want to achieve with your website. If you are using a website designer (which I did, as they are awesome) keep in mind that they are usually artists first, and businesspeople second. This means that their job is to make a very visually appealing website, but not necessarily a fully-functioning information and sales site. What you want to aim for is to have all of your business information available, and the ability to book or sell clients right from your site.

When creating a website, you want your message and branding to be strong. Branding is, as mentioned earlier, your business name, logo colours and tagline. Then, you will need some pictures of you doing your thing, pictures of your certifications, of you with famous people, or whatever you think that people give a crap about, and use that content on your website to show that you know what you are doing. Plus, you should also link any videos, blogs or awards you have to the site as well.

Your website should be simple, easy to use, and always have a link directly to a sales portal (a sales portal being a place on the website where they can give you money). If you go to the KPC website at *<www.kpcombat.ca>* and take a look around ... ours is a little more complicated than I'd like, but it's a good template for a functioning business website. You're going to want to have an outside border template done, that shows up on every page, to either collect contact information or direct clients to a place to book your service. When they get to that landing page (and really all the pages on your site should be treated as landing pages) the place that they can book should be the first thing they see. You want to make it easy for people to purchase; people are often lazy and will leave a site that is too confusing.

Throughout your website, you want short, concise writing, arranged in what's called the reverse pyramid. The most important, basic information at the top, and then the more specific stuff on the bottom, further down the page. All of your major information should be "top of fold" (a reference to the days of newspapers, where the most important news appeared on the front page, above the fold). I am in the process right now of going through our website copy, to make it shorter and more concise, to get people better understanding what's going on.

The more questions that can be answered on your website, the better. You may hear the opposite, for instance, that you shouldn't list prices on your website, in an attempt to generate contacts. To be honest, this method only works if you are a great salesperson and you have a lot of time to invest in sales. As an entrepreneur, you're already trying to do fifty things at once; writing programs, maybe you're in the middle of writing a book and filming videos and doing everything you can to get your business out there. Your time is valuable! The reason I like to have as much information as possible on the website, is because that then gets rid of the people who aren't really interested in what we're doing anyway. They have all the info, so if they do contact you, that lead is very strong, conversion is easy and you're not eating up time trying to convince people. Being busy and being productive are two different things.

Your website should have descriptions of what you do, a description of you as the owner, and it should have multiple contact methods. If you look at our website, on the bottom corner we have all the social media sites tagged there; LinkedIn, Facebook, Instagram, YouTube, and Twitter (even though I hate Twitter so much). These badges show people that they can search for you on various popular websites, and it gives them extra trust in your brand, knowing that they can research you on multiple different "impartial" websites.

Whether you are using a website designer or not, you want your website to be created on a content management system (CMS) you can work with. The content management system is the software your website is built on. A user-friendly content management system means you don't need to keep paying your web designer to do edits to the site. You can edit almost everything on the site yourself using the CMS, minus massive physical changes to the website like changing colours, borders, banners, that kind of major design stuff. All the other day-to-day stuff should be done by you - that way you're not constantly being billed by your website designer to keep having your stuff updated - until of course you can shuffle this off to someone else. Having an updated website is incredibly important, especially when it comes to SEO. We use Wordpress; it's so simple that even I get it!

The next step is to get the site out there to as many people as possible. The best way to accomplish that is with social media.

13 HOW TO MARKET WITH SOCIAL MEDIA
(Consideration: Funnel Level 3)

Social media is probably one of the most underrated and least-understood tools on the Internet, especially when it comes to marketing and advertising. A lot of people think that if they just get a Facebook page, and then open a Twitter account, people will start flooding in through the doors. I find that people either spend way too little or way too much on their social media marketing.

At KPC, we definitely use social media heavily. Facebook is by far our number one advertiser. We use it a lot for messages, and speed of communication; we use it to get out deals and products, and all that stuff. The point of this book is to give you a base understanding of all of the different tools that you have available, and to get your business up and running for as little money as possible. Ideally, by the end of this book, your major investment in your business will have been the book itself!

I consider the three most important social media outlets to be Instagram, LinkedIn, and Facebook.

(Yes, I know, the almighty Twitter is not on this list, and there is a reason - I hate it! It is the only platform where we seem to get no reception or response. Content that kills on other platforms fails on stupid Twitter! Anyways, I am sure plenty of people are good at working with it, but I am not. So, Twitter is out of my book! Take that, social media dictator!)

What is the whole point of social media? Why even use it? The easiest answer I can give you is - trust. Social media is the best way to build trust and knowledge in your brand. The more people are seeing you and hearing from you and reading your content, the more they are getting to "know" you. The more they know you, the more likely they will be to buy from you. Building trust and relationships is the key to all business, and social media is one of the most powerful ways to do that!

Here is where the first chapters of this book come in again. You have to know your message, and who you are speaking to, or you are going to have a bad time on social media. You need to know yourself, and what you want to accomplish, so people can see that uniformly across your social media presence. That will make people trust you and want to work with you.

Gone are the days of hiding your best stuff to keep it secret and special. People want to know what they are getting into, they want that free sample ...without actually taking a free sample. CrossFit is a great example of this. They literally give away a workout every day, every three days - for free - on their main site. Has this affected their business? Not a bit! People trained with it, and then wanted more. If your stuff is good and looks fun, then giving it away won't keep people away, it will bring them in.

Facebook
Facebook is by far the biggest social media outlet. As of the third quarter of 2016, Facebook had 1.79 billion active monthly users. For us, right now, it is the hub of all of our social media marketing. As of this writing, we have just hit two thousand "likes" on our Facebook page[9] (please feel free to like that page, as well as my Randy King Live page[10]!). We use Facebook for everything - content sharing, client interaction, promotion of events ... all of the things!

---

[9] https://www.facebook.com/KPCmartialarts/
[10] https://www.facebook.com/RandyKingLive/

Facebook is your multitool for social media. It's the most prominent and most popular social media outlet, so when you are promoting general things, Facebook should be your first port of call. You'll by far get the most reach this way. Facebook also has the best pay-per-click (PPC) mechanics on it (though Facebook also bought Instagram, so their metrics are getting pretty decent as well). Facebook is great because they keep making it great! You will want to spend a lot of time on there getting your community going. There is no better social media source right now for community building than Facebook.

Facebook gives you a couple of options. You can have a group page, you can have a fan page, and you can have your personal account. I highly recommend separating your personal account from your business account. For instance, for me, most of the stuff on my personal Facebook page is shares of my daughter and Batman stuff; my customers don't need to see that. Your customers may like you and if you want to make them your friend, and have them be exclusively on there, that's great, but you definitely want to make sure that your business stuff is your business stuff, and your personal stuff is your personal stuff.

You don't need an ex-lover going on your page freaking out and posting about how you are inadequate in the bedroom for all of your students to see, right? Maybe you don't have those problems, but I definitely used to. Wait - not the bedroom problems, of course - I meant the lady problems.

For the business side of things, there are two options; a group page and a fan page. A group page is fantastic for quick messages to your students. You can make a private group for your students so that you can instantly transmit information to all of them in one go, so your guys know when classes are being cancelled, etc. The second option is the fan page. I highly recommend a fan page for Facebook. It is like a regular account, with a profile picture, but it also gives you business-specific tools like calls to action, sign-ins, "book now" buttons, and more. You can advertise from that page through pay-per-click (which is very very important especially on Facebook). You can have unlimited followers on it, unlike a personal Facebook account which now is capped at five thousand followers, and unlike a group which I think stops at five hundred. All of these features make a fan page ideal for where to put all your business stuff. If you've separated yourself into two businesses like I have, Randy King Live and KPC Self Defense, then you're going to want two separate fan pages. Know your message, and know what you're putting on each page. For instance, my Randy King Live page has all my seminar information, while my KPC Self Defense page has blogs and videos.

Once you have your fan page up, you have the ability to make posts and share content. You're going to share whatever kind of content you've decided on, because without creating content, having the page is pointless. Don't neglect sharing other people's content too, if you see something really awesome. For example, if you see one of my rants and you love it, feel free to share that on your page - everybody benefits from that. Number one, you look like you're open-minded, because you're showing other people's stuff (especially if their stuff is similar to yours). Number two, these other places are creating content for you, so it makes things easier on your end. We share lots of blogs - I share Kasey Keckeisen's Budo Blog[11] all the time. I take memes from other sites, I share a lot of Tony Blauer's[12] stuff, I share a lot of Rory Miller's stuff, because trying to keep up posting fresh content can be tough.

Understand that every time you put a post up on a fan page, only about five percent of your fans are going to see that page. We have two thousand people on our Facebook page, so, quick math on that, only a hundred people are going to see each post I put up. Why? The reason is because that's how Facebook makes money. From your personal page, everyone who is "following" you will see your posts in their newsfeed. But from a business page, only five percent of people are going to get any one of your posts on their newsfeed. That means that you might have to pay to

---

[11] http://practicalbudo.blogspot.ca/
[12] http://www.tonyblauerblog.com/

circulate each post you make. The alternative is to encourage people to check in on your page by keeping it fresh. If you put posts up all the time, people will start checking your page all the time, so you don't have to always pay extra money to circulate your posts. That being said, chances are you're still going to want to boost posts on occasion.

Boosting a post is only worth it when you can get a return on the investment. For example, we have t-shirts now available through Spreadshirt[13]. We have t-shirts for all of our projects; Talking to Savages, Randy's Rants, KPC, Randy King Live. All of our t-shirts are on this website for dropship, and I put up a link as soon as all the shirts became available, and I boosted that post. I decided to boost that post for seven dollars, because for every shirt that I sell, eight dollars goes to me. On a seven-dollar boost, if I sell even one shirt from that, I've made my money back. From that advertisement, I sold six shirts, so obviously that seven-dollar boost gave me a good return on my investment. Knowing that, when you boost something, make sure any post you promote has a return on the investment, so it's going to be some kind of income-generating service. Whether it's a seminar, event, classes or product - those are the only ones you should be paying to boost.

It's easy to fall into the habit of paying for all of your posts, because it's going to seem super important for everyone to see everything you post. Maybe your school was in the paper. Maybe you were on your local breakfast television show, your local morning show, maybe you're a personal trainer and you went to the park and they decided to interview you. You're thinking "oh my God, this is so big, and I <u>have</u> to share this", and then you're going to want to boost the post. I recommend that unless you have a great advertising budget, and you're really good with money, do not boost any posts you have no potential to directly get money back from. Brand awareness and people knowing you exist is great, especially when you start out, but you can tank your

---

[13] https://shop.spreadshirt.ca/KPCSelfDefense

business by spending too much money advertising in the wrong places. If you won't make money back on it, do not boost the post. If you need to send instant information to your students, e-mailing is better for everybody. You should have a contact list for that anyways, or, again, start a Facebook group.

Quick guide for Facebook:
- start a group or a fan page (groups are more interactive)
- message and link up with people in your field
- create a following for your page - get likes
- make the page fun and relevant to what you do
- create ads from that page that link to your sales portals
- boost content that is doing well so you reach more people with your best stuff

Instagram
Instagram is for pictures and pictures only; you can't really sell on Instagram. Instagram is more for brand awareness and brand recognition, and less for hard selling. For example, you cannot link out from Instagram posts or share other posts. Instagram is for image-building, and for showing samples of what you do; pictures of your seminars, events, awards or whatever. So, if you go to our @kpcselfdefense Instagram page[14], you'll see my "US Marshal" coin, you'll see me teaching at Violence Dynamics in Minneapolis (if you can, you should go!), clips from our classes, and so on. We also use Instagram for contests and that kind of stuff, it's a really fun way to do updates. There are lots of filters and fun stuff to do - you can find a filter that works for you and use that consistently to create your brand, or you can mix and match, doesn't matter.

The engagement on Instagram is great, but the numbers on there, a bit like Facebook likes, are not that important. As long as you reach the right people that's good. Having more followers looks better, people will believe you are better because everyone wants to work with popular people. The more people that follow you, the better, but don't get too hung up on numbers - numbers are just

---

[14] https://www.instagram.com/kpcselfdefense/

an ego inflation game. I have two thousand fans on Facebook, but I do not have even ten percent of those people training at my gym. Understand that just because people "like" something, that doesn't mean a whole lot ... "liking" something is easy, doing something is hard. Especially in our line of business, where we're getting you off the couch and into shape or making you eat things you don't want to eat or do things you don't want to do, putting you in uncomfortable positions ... that requires more dedication than it takes to punch a "like" button. Having a lot of likes doesn't translate to income, and having a lot of income doesn't translate to a lot of likes. You need and want both of those things, a nice balance in-between.

LinkedIn
LinkedIn is a professional database. The way it was described to me before I started using it was: Facebook is for people who make eighty thousand dollars a year and under, and LinkedIn is for people who potentially make eighty thousand dollars a year and over. I don't think that's really the case; I think a lot of people are on LinkedIn because it's a great place to sell your professional work.

LinkedIn is for more serious, professional-looking content. On LinkedIn, I'm not going to share a meme of Yoda fighting Darth Vader in a KPC shirt - that's better suited for an Instagram post. On LinkedIn, I share seminar information, I share blogs, I share rants; all my professional image stuff. On my LinkedIn we just focus on the Randy King Live aspect, because it's me as a professional doing my thing, as opposed to KPC which is is our gym community and involves all of the instructors, as well as myself.

Know what social media platform your content is best suited for. If you get a good picture, you can put it on almost everything, but Instagram is more fun for people to engage with. Facebook is for pretty much everything; updates on your classes, basic selling, using pay-per-click to advertise. LinkedIn is for professional content; seminars and products, for example.

I know all of this sounds like A LOT to handle. You are probably wondering, on top of all the other things you have to do in a day, how will you manage this monster? Well, fear not! I have included an example of a basic social media marketing plan for you right here - I wouldn't leave you hanging!

Example Social Media Marketing Plan

This marketing plan makes use of three social media platforms; your Facebook fan page, Instagram, and LinkedIn. Each one of these sites fulfills different parts of our marketing needs, and, based on the research I have done, each is also optimized by using a certain number of posts in a given time period.

We will also be using three types of content creation to share, on top of using other people's shareable media and quotes. I want to make sure that we are optimizing social media, without over-saturating and in turn losing people's interest.

Content:

Blogs: (if you like to write) We will be releasing two blogs a week to help educate and promote. Blogs and Rants will be our major sources of content.

Videos: We will be aiming to release one of these a week, year-round. When one is not released, just re-share one of the existing rants.

Memes: We are producing memes every week. These are very marketable, and they will contain a "Randyism"; something I say all the time. These will also be the lead on much of the Randy King Live marketing.

These three types of content will make up the majority of our original content. The rest of our social media marketing campaign will rely on re-sharing other people's blogs, videos, and infographics, which will fill in the gaps in the number of posts that we need.

Frequency of posting:
The latest market research says that you should post content to

    Facebook: 2 times daily
    Instagram: 3 times daily
    LinkedIn: 1 time daily
    Blogs: twice a week
    YouTube: once a week

#Hashtags: A lot of people do not know what the point of hashtags are. Very simply, they are a quick way to link info across multiple social media sites. Anything you create or put up on your own should have the hashtag #KPC, and anything you post that involves me should have the tag #randykinglive. This way, your post links to all the other information we put out, and it also helps Google and YouTube link to the videos. You can create personal hashtags as well to link all your content for your students ... just make sure the hashtag is not already taken. Also, each weekday from Monday-Thursday has its own hashtag that I want you to use in the posts you make on that day.

Time investment: I only want you spending about 45 minutes, 5 days a week on social media, between sharing, responding to comments and making comments on other people's stuff. Included is a sample schedule (the one I will be following here in Edmonton) - you can follow it if you want, or if, for example, you don't want to use one of the platforms like LinkedIn, then just adjust. It is very easy for social media to take over your life! With this plan you will get maximum benefit for minimum effort.

Schedule: Each day, Monday through Friday, you should spend, as I said, about 45 minutes doing social media marketing. You can easily do less, but this is the most bang for your buck. Most of the content will be shared on all of the platforms, the table shows where the content will fit the best. It also lines up with that daily hashtag.

Social Media Marketing Schedule

MONDAY	Daily hashtag: **#mememonday**		
Facebook	KPC meme	KPC blog	x
Instagram	KPC meme	Class action shot	Video
LinkedIn	KPC blog	x	x
TUESDAY	Daily Hashtag: **#tuesdaymotivation**		
Facebook	KPC video	Outside blog/video	x
Instagram	Outside pic	Class pic	Class video
LinkedIn	KPC video	x	x
WEDNESDAY	Daily Hashtag: **#wednesdaywisdom**		
Facebook	Outside pic	Outside blog/video	x
Instagram	Outside pic	Related pop culture	Class pic
LinkedIn	Link back to site	x	x
THURSDAY	Daily Hashtag: **#throwbackthursday**		
Facebook	Old KPC blog	Old KPC video	x
Instagram	Old KPC pic	Old KPC pic	Old video
LinkedIn	Old KPC blog	x	x
FRIDAY	Daily Hashtag: explore new ones		
Facebook	KPC blog	Outside video	x
Instagram	Outside meme	Funny meme	Promo pic
LinkedIn	KPC blog	x	x

Like I have said, "content is king"! Make your own or share someone else's - just get the conversation going.

So, to wrap this up, social media is actually pretty easy. It sounds like a lot of work, but it's not. Number one is content creation; we will talk more about that in Part 3 of this book. Decide what you want to create, because if there is no content to share, there's no point in even having Facebook, Instagram, or LinkedIn. Content creation is first, that should be your first priority.

Whatever you are creating - videos, blogs, podcasts, photos - it doesn't matter. You need to figure out what your voice is, figure out how you differ from your teacher, how you differ from me, how you differ from everybody. What makes you, *you*. Why will people train with you over everybody else? If you are already teaching, there are people training with you right now that chose you over everyone else … why? Saying that it's because you're "the best" is not true - there are so many better out there, there's no such thing as "best". If I have learned anything from the UFC in 2015/16, it is that anybody can be beaten. There is no "best", it's about people finding someone they like and trust. Everybody finds an instructor because they either want to be like them or they want to gain something from them. So, what is the thing that people want to gain from you? Make that your voice. (I chose rants, because I like to talk!) Once you have the content creation going, use it strategically. All professional content - LinkedIn. All fun, short stuff - Instagram. All of it also goes onto your Facebook page, and then market it, market it, market it.

14 SALES
(Purchase: Funnel Level 6)

Every time I talk to a new business owner, they usually tell me the same thing - "I suck at sales." Everyone seems to think sales is this complex mechanism, full of tricks and body language reading, and all these "mystic" things that you can learn for $15.95. I think the most succinct way to explain sales is with a quote I heard a long time ago. I don't remember who exactly it came from, but it was, "*Sales is just enthusiasm transferred*". That's the essence of sales. If you're pumped about the thing you're selling, you're going to be able to sell it. Every human being every day is a salesperson. They sell going to the movie they want to see, little kids sell staying up late, or getting the toy they want. You've been in a position your whole life where you've done sales, you just haven't classified it in your brain that way, so you just assume you're bad at sales.

Most people are bad at <u>cold</u> sales. Luckily, since you're an entrepreneur, and you're selling something that you love, your enthusiasm should automatically be in it, and you will instantly become an amazing sales person.

Obviously, selling is an art, and there are ways to get better, but the number one part of it is that your enthusiasm has to transfer. You have to be excited about what you do, and then that has to come across in your product. That enthusiasm, that ability, that love you have, needs to transfer when you're talking to people. I'm going to go over a bunch of jargon in this chapter, but understand that the basic premise is that if you've ever asked a person out on a date, or if you've ever made somebody see a movie or watch a TV show they didn't want to watch, you have successfully completed a sale. The stakes were just lower, because there was no money involved. That's the major difference between the everyday interactions which are actually still sales, and then the sales transactions at your location. Put the idea that you're a bad salesperson right off the table. You are not bad at sales, you've just never considered much of what you do to be sales.

Even if sales were an entirely new and alien thing, learning the art of the sale is a good thing! You need the dedication to improving yourself in order to improve your business.

The central notion of this book, of "selling out to your level of comfort", is very important here. There will be times when you're not going to want to do hard sales, or you're not going to want to pressure people into training with you, and I totally understand that. I firmly believe that the people that train with you should start with you because they *want* to start with you, not because they were tricked into it, or scared into it. They should stay with you because they choose to stay with you, not because you have a contract over their head, or because there's some other reason. If they want to buy from you, they should buy from you willingly, and they should stay with you willingly as well. It shouldn't be a trick or a scam, right?

Tell people why you do what you do. Tell them your story. People love to hear your story, especially in the business of client-based sales. We want to have people coming over and over and over again. If they know your story, and they feel like a part of your life, they're going to be more inclined to buy.

Tell people why you opened a gym - don't undersell your competitors or say negative things - but tell them why you decided not to go work at Mom's Yoga, why you wanted to open your own gym. Tell people about your travels and your experiences, and people are going to respond to that. They're going to see your passion for this, and they're going to jump on board. It is incredible what we as humans can normalize. You may have told your story so many times that you are sick of it, but the world isn't sick of it - most people have still not even heard it once.

In sales, I find people have a problem with two things: they don't want to ask for money (or anything else for that matter, such as reviews), and they don't want to annoy people. In the game we're playing, you will have to collect money, and you will have to "annoy" people by asking them things multiple times.

If you don't collect money, you're never going to have any money to pay your bills, and your business is going to shut down. You have to immediately get comfortable accepting money from people, especially friends. Understand that yeah, you love what you do, but as in the pricing chapter where we talked about how to price yourself, you should understand what you're worth, and know that your time is important. Your time needs to be valued, because if clients are just coming in because of discounted rates, they're not going to be great clients.

You also have to get comfortable with repeating yourself. *Old-timey sales stat alert!!* For most sales, it takes somebody hearing or seeing something approximately seven times before that thing becomes top-of-mind. (You want your business to be top-of-mind, as that means that they are likely to think of you when they want to buy.) Get used to repeating yourself - *a lot.* Let's say you mention an upcoming workshop. Due to the fact that you are so pumped about this workshop, you're going to remember mentioning it even after just one time. However, remember that you are not your clients. Unless you're doing a hell of a job, they are not going to be as super pumped about your product as you are, they will need constant reminders. This happens to me all the time; I say things and people don't hear them ... and I am LOUD!! When I am making an announcement about an upcoming seminar, for what must be the fiftieth time, without fail someone will be shocked to hear this information. I <u>know</u> I have spoken about the seminar fifty times - I say it at the end of every single class - but sometimes people just don't listen; they zone out, or they're tired. You've got to keep this stuff in people's faces, many will need to hear it multiple times. Lesson one, then, is that what *you* might consider extremely annoying (repeating yourself *ad nauseum*) might just be a reminder for others. <u>Always</u> follow up.

Lesson two, you have to understand that while "no" obviously means "no" in a self-defense situation ("no" means "no" for a lot of things), in sales, most people's first "no" is just a reactionary "no". I'm not telling you to sell, sell, sell, and keep harassing people, what I'm saying is that you need to keep people informed all the time. If you're talking to a client and mention "Hey, I thought you were signing up for our intro trial session this week" and the client responds with "nah, I can't because of this, this, and this" - don't take that "no" as a negative. Every single "no" has a reason behind it; there's a purpose to that "no". Often people will stop at that "no", and then they don't even know what the actual issue was. Maybe you get a hold of somebody, and they are against coming in to your location ... but then you find out it's because they don't have any money, or because they just went through a divorce, or because something else happened in their life. Does that mean they never want to train with you? Usually no. Even after that first rejection, if they can't use your service, right now, that should not be the end of the conversation. Ask them more questions and get as much information as you can! I won't lie to you, sometimes they really just don't want your service ... but that is actually much rarer than you would think. Not every "no" turns into a "yes", but if you want to find out the true objection you need to keep the conversation going. Here is an example:

> *Owner*: "Hey so I got your email, sounds like you want to start up, when do you want to come down? I have an opening Monday at 6 and Tuesday at 1."
>
> *Client*: "No, I can't train this cycle."

Most people might end the conversation right there. But if you add just a couple more things, you could change the outcome.

> *Owner*: "Oh no, I hope everything's ok ... if you don't mind me asking, how come?"

Client: "Oh, I forgot that I have school the same nights as class." (if the reason is too personal or the person is very private they may not answer, but again rare)

Owner: "Ah, that makes sense. Well, is it all right if we keep you up to date on our programs?"

Client: (either yes or no)

It is pretty simple to get more information, just follow a basic rule of three. Don't give up on one "no", but don't push past three either. Just going through the process of getting a "no" once, then the second "no", and then asking for further contact from that point forward is just such a huge benefit; it helps keep your lead pool filled.

Once you ask for follow-up contact, many times they will respond, "ok, for sure, get a hold of me, maybe I'll be more interested in another event". Maybe two or three years down the road, you're going to get somebody coming back in. It constantly shocks me. We've been in business going on nine years in October ... we have people still coming back from 2008 and 2009, that haven't trained with us for years. Out of the blue they want to pop back in because now their kids are grown up, or life has slowed down, they've changed jobs, etc. We have people coming in and out all the time.

Get used to the fact right now that you will be talking to people multiple times, who have still not bought from you yet. There's going to be so many times where you see the same person over and over again, and you thought they were going to sign up and they didn't. It might get frustrating, but if they have not outright told you that they are never coming in, don't stop. Remember that this is a tactic that should be used on the leads you gain from my system, where the leads have contacted you first (so at one point they wanted to do business with you). This is not a tactic to use on random people you meet at a party.

I have said it before, and I'll say it till I'm dead - you should always be tracking. (This is something that I struggle with, because I am a big-picture person, not a small details person.) At every point in time when a customer is in contact with you, for a potential sale, you should have some kind of mechanism to track the entire process, whether it's a purchase mechanism for sales like a sales tracking program, or whether it is something you've created of your own design, you should be tracking that whole process. What I mean by that is there should be a record of your interactions. If they call you, there should be a phone log. If they email you, there should be an email log. If they catch you on Facebook, you should be logging all this and keeping it in one place, so you can constantly keep going back and looking at it. Where a lot of businesses suffer, and we went through this as well, is in letting people slip through the cracks. Maybe a mom called you one day, and wanted to sign up her four kids for your service. She was super pumped about it, and so were you, but in all that excitement, you forgot to take down her information. Then if there is no further contact, a lot of people take it personally and assume that she just didn't want the service after all. Yes, it could be that she didn't want the service ... or it could be that because she has four kids, she got super busy, and then something else popped up, and she forgot which person she called. If you had been able to do a follow-up call, along the lines of "hey, so you gave us a call last week, I was wondering if you still want your kids signed up!", ninety percent of the time, on that second contact, you're going to get a confirmation. Often you are the only one who actually cared enough to call back, and now they know that they're not just money to you. They feel there is a relationship being built; plus it shows you have excellent customer service, and that always goes a long way.

So, you should always be tracking, and you should always be following up on leads until the leads close. A lead is only closed when they tell you, "hey, we're done, I don't want to do this anymore", like, "I'm never going to come there, I signed up with another gym, I don't like you period" - they're gone. Say the person moves, well, they're gone as well. Until that point, though, once every couple of weeks you should be looking at your leads with the mindset that, "Hey, all those people that emailed us during our last promotion, only three of them came in. On our next promotion, let's get them in". This is where your tracking is going to come in exceptionally handy. I cannot stress enough that you need to follow up on stuff ... don't harass, just ask.

You should have some kind of mass communication system, for classes and for internal sales. This could be a Facebook group, and/or an email list ... preferably both. We have a Facebook group that is just for current students, as a lot of the seminars we sell only apply to existing clients. The Facebook group really helps us stay in contact with everyone and allows anyone who is currently registered to share inside stuff, tips and tricks, videos and they can also talk about class stuff. This creates a bigger and better culture, a group dynamic where everybody feels like they're part of the same team. That sense of community will help get people who stick around.

Using email for marketing is on its way out, although email is still a good way to keep in contact with your customer base. It takes a lot of time to create content for your email marketing lists, and also, people are starting to see email marketing as interruption marketing, or digital junk mail. That being said, you should still have an email list of every client you have ever had contact with. Getting an old client back takes one-third the investment it takes to create a new one, so keep contact and always follow up. You can either run the email list yourself through a free service (if you do it this way make sure people have a way to opt out) or you can use a paid email service. We recently upgraded to MailChimp. I love them as a service so much that I pay the monthly fee ... even though it is free for up to five hundred contacts. You should be collecting emails every chance you get, and there should be a place on your website where people can sign up for your list. The main reason I am still using and paying for email marketing is that in the paid service, I have the ability to send out automatic emails. As soon as someone signs up for the list, they get eight emails over a period of time informing them about what we do. I personally don't have a lot of time for email marketing, so I don't put a lot of faith into it, but some people run huge businesses on it. Like everything in this book, you should try it out even if I am not a fan. You may find that it is the best way for you to communicate!

That's your basic Sales 101. Understand that money is part of every transaction, you just have to accept that. Remember you've been a salesperson your whole life, you just never equated it to sales (so don't tell me you're not good at sales). Sales is mostly just enthusiasm transferred; getting somebody else pumped to do the thing that you're pumped about. Understand that "no" might not always mean "no" in this sales game - "no" might mean "maybe" ... don't become the crazy harsh salesperson, but keep communicating and double checking. Get the "no", explore the "no", and then, if that "no" is firm, ask for follow-up contact. Ask for the appointment, then ask for the sale. Keep on top of following up, and your client base will keep growing.

PART THREE

LONGEVITY AND CULTURE

15 CONTENT CREATION

When it comes to internet marketing, you are going to need to produce content on an ongoing basis. Content can be anything from blogs, to videos, to podcasts. The more content you have, the better the picture of you and your business that is available out there for potential and existing clients to get.

In the words of social media expert Gary Vaynerchuck[15]: "content is king, but context is God".

Not to beat a dead horse, but before you start making your content, you need to know one thing. You guessed it - your message. All the content you create should line up with what you are trying to do. Understand that content creation is not a direct sale. It is more of a soft sell, more about getting the word out and positioning yourself as a trusted expert, and less about trying to convert sales. The marketing point of social media is to get as much content out there as possible. We have our Randy's Rants[16], which I'd love to say come out weekly, but you know that's a lie. On top of that, we do a podcast[17] and a blog[18]. All of

---

[15] https://www.garyvaynerchuk.com/
[16] http://kpcombat.ca/randys-rants
[17] http://randykinglive.com/podcast
[18] http://kpcombat.ca/blog

the things that we put out there help to generate traffic for our website and social media, which then helps potential clients decide if they are picking up what I am putting down! A strong internet presence helps lend credibility to a business as well - just because the tools have changed does not mean marketing has. The more places you are seen, the more weight people will put behind your words.

Content creation sounds like a very overwhelming process, but really it's not. The best thing to do, which I call the "author approach", is to make one area your content creation hub. For us, Randy's Rants are our major content creation; I put all my priority into filming the rants. From that strong base, you can then convert that work into other media. We converted rants into blogs - so now I've killed two birds with one stone. Some people prefer to read, some people prefer to watch videos, and now I can access both kinds of people. Although statistically, the videos are crushing it, some people still like to have that blog experience, like to read stuff, read over it again, and have that to research and refer back to. Some people just might not like the tone of your voice, the way you speak or whatever, and so a blog might be a better way to get your thoughts out. From those blogs, we can compile an ebook. Ideally, that's my plan next; after this book, I will be putting out a book called "Still Ranting", all about my views on self-defense and what I think is different about my thoughts and theories on how self-defense works (you should totally buy it). So, in the same way that an author writes a book, and then once they write the book they go on a book tour, and then after the book tour they make a movie - it's all the same content. Content creation doesn't have to be overwhelming. You just have to make content that can be shared over multiple platforms. Create that brand, create that one thing ... then reuse the poop out of it.

Randy's Rants have been blogs, articles for magazines, and even a seminar tour! The seminar tour started off with just three dates, but because I named it the "Randy's Rants Rockstar Tour", people started watching the rants. During the rants we promoted the seminars, and not only did we grow from three seminar locations to eight in just three months, I more than doubled engagement with the rants, thanks to all the bookings.

What kind of content should you make? Make whatever you enjoy, or whatever you are best at. The reason we did the rants is because I am not a strong writer. I don't have the passion for writing, it doesn't relax me, I don't have that writer's thing where there's a thought in my head and I have to get it out and put it on paper. When I have to get things out, I have to get them out verbally. My friend Dillon Beyer told me there was no way I would ever be a better writer than I am a presenter, and I had to agree. My personality is better in real life, so instead of struggling with the writing, I just grabbed a video camera. Create stuff that is true to you, not just something that can go "viral". Make sure that people can share your content, and ask them to often, especially the influencers in your field. In the old days, you needed a book or a show to become well-known. Now you just need a webcam or a microphone. Take advantage of that!

You'll also need to find a place to host all of your content. Most people use their website for a lot of their hosting, but it is way more powerful to use an outside free service to do it, that way some of your promotion is already done for you. It would be ridiculous if you were creating videos and not putting them on YouTube; you never know who will see them there. Same thing with blogs and podcasts - host them on your site, but also share them on various podcast and blog sites. Some great places right now are SoundCloud, iTunes ... clearly YouTube is great for videos, but so is Vimeo. Blogs can be hosted on Tumblr or Blogspot. The goal is to get your content in front of as many eyes as possible - there are other methods than just Facebook.

Try not to let numbers and views deter you. The one reason to create free content is to funnel it into paid content. We don't have a lot of views, but our target demographic market is fantastic, because the people that are watching the videos are decision makers. If I get three hundred, four hundred, five hundred views, and if out of those five hundred views, two hundred are school owners that are potentially going to bring me in, then that's going to grow my business in the appropriate way.

When producing content, keep in mind that the more popular you get (especially on Facebook and YouTube) the more there will be people that are going to hate you - this is something that you're just going to have to get over. Matt Page (Master Ken from Enter the Dojo[19]) was in Edmonton for a seminar, and his line to me was, "Start a YouTube channel, and then never look at the comments". I think that's hilarious because he gets a lot of hate, but it's because he's popular. The more work you do, the better you get, the more popular you become. The more popular you are, the more eyes that will see your stuff, and more eyes means you are going to start running into people that don't agree with you. I want you to take that as a win.

The first time we got hate on my YouTube page was a day of celebration. That might sound crazy, but it meant that the video was going to places that I've never been. If everybody likes what you're saying, that means you're just talking to the same people all the time. You're just talking to people you know, you're just talking to people that are friends of those people. Once you get that first hater, though, and they really attack you for what you're saying and doing, that means you've made it! You've made it!

There's no celebrity that everybody likes, there is no human being that everybody's going to agree with, you could be the smartest person in the world and people are going to disagree with you. You can be the most popular person in the world and some people are still going to hate you, that's just the way it is. If you start polarizing people, that means you're popular. That means your stuff is getting to new places. Your marketing is working, because now people that you've never talked to are seeing your stuff.

There's no such thing as bad publicity, people say this all the time, and this is especially true with content on social media. When people are freaking out on you, hating on you, sharing your stuff in a negative light ... this is actually good as long as your content is not b.s. How? Well, everyone has other people following them. This is called a "natural market", and it's something you're going

---

[19] https://www.youtube.com/user/EnterTheDojoShow

to want to break into. Getting into the natural market is something social media is really, really good for.

The concept of a natural market is pretty simple. On average, if you died tomorrow, about seventy-five people are going to come to your funeral. Those people are your natural market. Each person knows about seventy-five people in their life that they engage with on a regular basis throughout the year; whether they are family, friends, work associates, etc. Normally, you want people who like you to share your stuff, so that their natural market can see you as well. However, let's say a super-popular human in your area hates your video and shares it, saying "this is such garbage, can you believe this???". Out of those average seventy-five people in their natural market, it's pretty much guaranteed that at least ten of those people *can't stand* that person. So, when someone shares stuff they hate, ten people in their natural market might just love it.

You need to get in front of as many people as possible ... but (spoiler alert) they won't all love you.

Example avenues of content creation

- blog, on your website or another
- podcasts
- videos
- web series
- video of your services
- question and answer sessions

16 SPONSORING ADS / WHAT IS PPC?

So your content is awesome now, and you have been reaching a lot of people. How do you make sure you are getting your best stuff in front of more eyes?

Well, if you have been doing this for a while, and if you have been posting all of your content on social media (as you should be) then Facebook in particular may have prompted you to sponsor some ads. People always ask me if they should do this. The answer is yes - but here are some tips, and also an explanation of how you pay for advertising on social media.

First of all, after you post some of your content on social media, do not sponsor it right away. The way Facebook works is that it wants to provide the best service for its users. With this in mind, Facebook will pitch you an initial price for sponsoring a post, but if your material gets a strong organic viewership (non-sponsored views) they will actually *lower* the price you would have to pay to promote it. I know this sounds crazy, but yes, Facebook will actually tell you which content people like better, and then will charge you *less* to get it out into the world! So, don't sponsor immediately. Post, share, link, and tag people, and if it starts getting traction, then spend money on it. Do not throw cash into your dud posts to get them more views - get your strongest stuff out there. Then, with some tracking, you can start to make more content similar to that.

So what does sponsorship mean? In essence it is really just a version of the most common method of advertising online, which is known as pay-per-click (PPC). PPC is everywhere, and it's probably the best bang for your buck, especially if you're just starting out. Pay-per-click is exactly what it sounds like. You create an ad or link, and then every time somebody clicks on it, you are charged an amount of money. The amount is decided in a manner along the lines of an online auction, so you can either take the amount they suggest, or pay a little more to ensure that your ad comes up. The company then advertises your content for you, targeting people you might not get naturally, and when one of them clicks, you pay. It's amazing, because you only end up paying for people who are interested. Facebook is your main player for this, and it is becoming increasingly difficult to get stuff out on Facebook without using PPC.

Here is where all these online business models start making money off of you - but the good news is you get to decide how much. PPC is a simple, interesting marketing method that is actually very lucrative, easy to use, intuitive, and can get pretty great results. Where this method fails is if the link you put up leads to a garbage page, which is why you need a good website. Each campaign might direct traffic to a different place, but all traffic should land on a sales page.

The most important and cost-saving method for PPC is knowing your demographic; who you are trying to train. If you know your demographic, you can target your PPC advertising and greatly reduce your costs. Many people make a huge mistake and shotgun this; they just spend as much money as possible and spread their message as widely as possible, and whoever comes is whoever comes ... don't do that! The game is not to get as many leads as you can, it is to get the *right* leads, for people that actually want what you have to offer.

The best analogy I have for this is the fisherman analogy. Many people will be telling you to be like a fisherman, and cast a huge net. You don't actually want to cast a huge net! You don't want to be fishermen, you want to be tuna fishermen. I want to cast a small, far less expensive net, and only get the fish that I am looking for, which is my demographic. My business demographic is twenty-five- to forty-year-old white-collar workers of all genders, so all of my advertising is directed towards those people. I make use of the fact that Facebook lets me select the specific audience I want to target, in an easy, step-by-step process. We are talking age, gender, interest, keywords searched (specific to Google AdWords), location ... and I am sure more categories will pop up the second this book is published. All of these fields help me reach the specific clients I am seeking, so the people that are seeing my ads are only the people I want. The people clicking it are the people that I *want* clicking it, which is a far stronger lead.

Main tips for PPC:

- use your best stuff, as determined by organic views
- when just advertising, know your demographic
- stick to your message

17 BEING ALLERGIC TO OVERHEAD

There are three main things most businesses tend to fail on. Number one, they don't have a strategic plan on how to grow, or if they do grow, they don't have a plan for how to cope. Number two, the person gets bored, because they are doing things they don't want to do (more on that in the next chapter). Number three, which we will focus on in this chapter, the bills start piling up so high that it runs the business right into the ground.

Everything you do to improve your business is going to require some kind of investment. One-time investments are different from overhead; a one-time investment is a one-time cost, while overhead is ongoing. Any equipment you bring in (unless you are leasing), signs, paint, etc., are one-time investments, and not considered overhead. Most of your building/renovation costs are not considered overhead, unless you need to pay to maintain them. Overhead is a recurring bill that you're going to be paying month-to-month to keep the business running.

I have a saying that I'd like to get into your head, which is that you need to be "allergic to overhead". As soon as you become a business owner, it seems like it is the job of every other company in the world to get money out of your pocket. They're going to want to sell you management software, and bookkeepers, and lawyers, and you're going to need to file taxes, and you're going to need to be on websites, there's going to be SEO talks, there's going to be people asking for your cash in order to grow their own business or to cross-promote.

When I first opened KPC, I had just come off a divorce. I was living in my friend's basement, I had no car, no credit card debt, no insurance. Other than child support, I had no bills. As KPC grew, I bought a nicer vehicle, had a credit card, bills started piling up. Every time we've been in financial distress at KPC, it's always been a result of the overhead.

There's acceptable overhead and unacceptable overhead, just like there is acceptable debt and unacceptable debt. That twenty thousand dollars you racked up gambling in Vegas is unacceptable debt, but the loan you took to buy your house is acceptable debt. The same is true with overhead.

So, let's talk "acceptable" overhead. The two biggest components of your acceptable monthly overhead are salary and infrastructure costs (rent on space, cost of server space, etc.). At the beginning, you just want to keep these two costs as low as possible, especially if you are bootstrapping. You're going to be tempted to get a spot in a very nice neighbourhood, with the idea that *because* you're in a nice neighbourhood, people will flock to your location, and those people will also have more money. Location, location, location is the standard mantra when people talk about real estate investing - but you're not investing in real estate here, you're investing in your business. Starting off in a crappy part of town, being in the basement, being upstairs, but paying a little less overhead, is probably your best move, unless you're opening a multiple-investor gigantic gym facility. Find a space that fits your needs, and understand how big your space needs to be and its basic requirements. Are your clients moving around a lot? How much storage do you need? Is the structure of the floor safe enough to drop weights on?

When you're opening a gym, for example, if you're starting from the ground up, you're not going to need a space of more than about a thousand square feet, plus an office. If you want change rooms or showers, that's obviously going to cost you more, but do you need those initially? Probably not. Most martial arts gyms survive without showers and change rooms, as long as there's a bathroom where people can change (or people can change ahead of time). All you're going to need is that open space. If you need an office on-site, that's obviously going to take up space as well.

At KPC we started our gym with nine hundred square feet, and eventually went up to fifteen hundred square feet in that original space. We're now in a new space, with thirteen hundred and fifty square feet, but in a better layout so it seems bigger. That's another factor to consider; how much of your square footage is usable? We run thirty to forty people in our space easily. As long as you know what you're doing and understand how to play with space, you can keep your overhead low on that.

Your lease is always going to be overhead. If you're subcontracting out, look for the place that charges the lowest hourly rate. You can rent a church basement or a community hall for a pretty decent rate to start.

As your business grows, your overhead will grow automatically, there's no way around it. If you're by yourself, renting community halls, eventually you're going to run out of room, and you're going to have to get bigger. Getting bigger means paying more money. Then, if you keep growing and you go full-time, you're going to need to pay yourself and maybe other people. Every time you hire an employee, your overhead's going to go up. Keeping costs down as much as possible is crucial - you need to be allergic to overhead.

A second acceptable type of overhead is paying for an accountant and a lawyer. Even if they're not on retainer (you can put them on retainer as a one-time cost) you definitely want to have them. A bookkeeper is not essential (if you keep on top of the books) but an accountant is a must. You need to make the time to put your accountant to good use. Sit down with them, pay the extra money for a chance to talk with them, and make sure you're both on the same page in order to keep your taxes as low as they can be.

Taxes are another acceptable type of overhead, and a huge one at that. Taxes are where your accountant is going to pay off. If you get a proper accountant that will find all the loopholes you're missing, they pretty much pay for themselves on what they save in taxes. Spend the money on the accountant, but then try to use their services only as much as is absolutely necessary.

The next item on your "acceptable overhead" list is your online presence; advertising, website, PayPal fees. You can use some free web services, particularly at the start, but you're eventually going to reach a point in your business where that no longer meets your needs.

Advertising should be a weekly overhead, and you should make sure it's within your budget. The only way this really becomes a negative is if you don't know how to target advertising (which you do by now, after reading the previous chapter). As your school grows, your advertising budget should grow as well, which will make the overhead go higher and higher. The good thing about advertising overhead is that you can get a good return on investment (ROI) from it, meaning that if you don't advertise, you're not going to get any more people in. How I like to do it is to set the amount of my advertising budget per campaign at the cost of one full-pay student. By this model, if your gym charges seventy-five dollars a month, you should be spending about seventy-five dollars a month in advertising. The first client you get from that advertising automatically pays it off. If you're getting twenty, thirty, forty people per advertising spot, spend a little bit more money on it. You're going to want to throw all your money at advertising because it's so important, but it's more important to pay your bills and not go broke. What if your advertising campaign doesn't work, what if you have to experiment with advertising, what if it hits the wrong people, what if your pay-per-click goes down, your posters don't work and you spend all this money? This is how businesses run themselves into the ground. Keep your advertising overhead as low as you reasonably can.

Let's talk now about unacceptable or non-mandatory overhead. As soon as you're online, somebody is going to call you and talk to you about a management system for your gym. Unless you're doing contract payments, and unless you are following the exact same formula as everybody else running a martial arts business or a personal training business, grabbing a MindBody or Rainmaker system is not for you. At KPC we don't use any of those systems. Did we lose clients in droves like they said we would? Nope. Until you're above fifty to sixty students, I don't see a reason for you to need either an administrative assistant or a program that manages your school. You should be able to handle that by yourself. Once you get to the point where your bills are paid, and you have some money in the bank, and you have extra on top of that, then by all means, go ahead, but don't get it unless you absolutely need it. Even if you're starting to feel overwhelmed, I'd probably still suggest hiring an administrative assistant part-time over getting the school-running software. I think it's great for businesses with three, four, five hundred clients, but not when you are still small and starting out.

As you go forward in your business, as you grow, your overhead will grow too. This is why you look at gyms that have seventy, eighty, a hundred people, and you think, "oh my goodness, this person must have so much money", but they probably don't. There's the cost of the janitor they had to hire because the place is too big for them to clean on their own, their accounting and bookkeeping costs are higher, and since they don't have time to do everything themselves they hired a company to do their social media.

If you can do anything in your business, do not increase your overhead until you're absolutely sure you can support that overhead. *Be allergic to overhead.* There are some things you have to pay - you have to pay your lease, you have to pay your website fees, you have to pay your freaking taxes - but for every other add-on service that sounds like a great idea, I highly recommend waiting at least two months to see if you can afford it, in case there is a dip in your income stream.

An important consideration to remember for all overhead is to be wary of entry offers. Many companies and services offer low entry prices for new customers, and just as you come to rely on them, they increase their fees or upsell you. So what you thought was going to be eighty dollars a month turns out to be two hundred.

18 KNOWING WHO YOU ARE

As far as I'm concerned, the point of opening a business is to do what you want to do, when you want to do it. Why would you open your own business in order to do a bunch of stuff you hate doing? Maybe you hate bookkeeping, maybe you hate advertising, maybe you hate sales. As an entrepreneur, your skill set is going to need to include almost all of these things (at least at first), but don't fall into the entrepreneur's trap of thinking that you're the only person that can do everything. You might be the one who can clean the gym the best, who teaches class the best, who answers the emails the best, but the point of having your own business is for you to be doing what you want to do, making money while you're doing it, and having an awesome life, living the dream that nobody else gets to live. You need to work with your strengths, and outsource your weaknesses. There are definitely going to be some places where you are better than anyone else … just not everywhere, and you need to be honest with yourself about this. Not everything will need your personal involvement. Just because you can build the best program, does not mean you are the best to teach it. Figure out where you excel, and then do everything in your power to make sure those things are the only things you need to do.

Your first three major hires should most likely be a lawyer, an accountant, and ideally, an administrative person as well. Lawyers and accountants need to be trained specialists. As for administrative work, it is just time-consuming. So much valuable time gets eaten up in responding to the same email day after day, and that time is better suited to making the business better.

A lot of people try to be everything to everybody, so you may think that as an entrepreneur you've got to be the best at everything. That is simply not true. Yes, at the beginning, you will be doing everything yourself, but as the heart of the company, your time is better spent on improving the brand as opposed to the daily workings. As an entrepreneur, you should always know at least a little about every part of your business, so that you can converse with contractors on an educated level. This will keep you from getting hosed over when you decide to move on or transfer it out, but you only need to be an expert in what you are trying to accomplish (not the day-to-day).

My strengths are teaching group classes, advertising, and just generally anything social. I am a very "big picture" person, not a small details person. This means that when it comes to small details, I roll my eyes, I get it done while grimacing, and I will find anything else in the world to do. My house is never cleaner than when I have to write, or when I have to do our taxes.

The first day I was able to hire somebody to run private lessons for me was one of the greatest days of my life! Private lessons were great unless I was feeling sick, or there was something going on where I couldn't feed off the energy in the room (as an extrovert, I am an energy vampire!). So, private lessons are not one of my favourite things to teach, and if we could make enough money with me not doing private lessons, I would not do them at all. That will be my success measure, when I can transfer off all of my daytime clients to another instructor, showing that a) we have enough money to hire additional people, and b) I don't have to do the stuff I don't want to do.

On the worksheet at the end of this chapter, you are going to list your strengths. Then, you are going to list your weaknesses. Both of these can be difficult, so to prime the pump, I will give you my strengths first, followed by my weaknesses, and then I will explain to you how I turned my weaknesses into strengths.

Strengths - *outgoing, likes to talk, loves meeting new people, likes helping, loves teaching, great in a crowd*

Weaknesses - *small details, writing, accounting, paying attention to income/output, keeping things on track, feast or famine mentality*

When I first started out, I had to learn to be better at my weaknesses, because there was no way around it. I will never be as good at my weaknesses as I am at my strengths, though. What I did, as KPC became more successful, was to hire people who are strong in the areas I am weak. I "wrote" most of this book via voice memo. Michelle (the saint, and the Hand of the King) who transcribed the memos for me was doing what she loved; she loves writing. So, I turned my weakness into a strength by finding a way to accomplish the things that I normally hate to do in a way that I enjoyed. I would rather talk than write, so doing it via voice memo was the smarter way to go. I got the output that I needed to get done, I'm creating the products that need to be created, but I'm not doing it in such a way that I end up dusting for the fifteenth time because I'd rather do that than write.

On the topic of dusting, another thing I don't like doing is cleaning our gym ... so we also got somebody to clean our gym. We had enough money to do it, so we outsourced the cleaning as well. All the things that you don't want to do or are not strong at, you should outsource. Any time you can free up so you can work from your strengths will just make your business stronger. Every hour I am not cleaning the gym or wiping mats or pads, every hour I am not stuck responding to the same email I've already responded to fifteen times, every hour I'm not procrastinating on writing - these are all hours I can be working on something productive like creating a rant, or voice-recording a book, or improving our curriculum, making new contacts, networking, or just building the business in the ways that I am the strongest. Build a team around you that will support you.

Worksheet 5 - Strengths and Weaknesses

Strengths:

Weaknesses:

19 BUILDING YOUR TEAM

When you're looking at building your team, you definitely want to have some opposites on there to complement each other. A lot of people think that aiming for similarities is great for strength, but while it may be great within departments, it is not as great for an organization.

Let's look at big business. Having a great sales team will only be good if you also have a great set of accountants, and a great manager, and great administrative assistants. It doesn't matter how small your organization is, you need to find people that are different from you, and strong in the areas you are not, in order to make things work.

Our private lessons instructor, my partner Thor, is a much more introverted person than I am. This works really well for the one-on-one aspect of private lessons. He is, I think, a better private coach than I am (even though he won't admit it because he's far too humble). His quiet attention to detail is perfect for many of the people who are looking to do private lessons. When I do private lessons, I'm all about the big picture stuff ... I want to show the client a whole bunch of different things so I don't get bored, and get them moving, where Thor is more methodical and focuses on the technical end. This is why we work so well as a team - I thrive on the large groups, and he prefers to handle the smaller, one-on-one stuff. Both of us could stand to increase our abilities in each area, so that the business can run smoothly when one of us is not there. However, playing to our strengths has made our business grow exponentially. Thor's skill at teaching private lessons, and the consistent income from the people that keep coming back to him, got us into a new, better space, and it got us the ability to start looking at opening a second location.

You definitely want to hire a staff that complements you. I am the king of the extroverts and Thor is the king of the introverts, and we work very well together. As in any workplace, in order to keep things working well, there needs to be a shared language. In order for it to work, the sales team has to be able to work with the accountants, even though they might not go for drinks afterwards. You can lead very separate lives but still work together fantastically as a team.

As your business grows, look for people who are suited to the areas that you want to give up. For instance, let's say that you excel at meeting people, but you want to have front-end staff. You're going to want to hire somebody close to your personality to do that for you. If you're looking for a second-in-command, you want to find somebody who has a perfect second-in-command mentality, so you don't shoot yourself in the foot.

A lot of people find and mentor people just like themselves - forgetting that they themselves left what they were doing to become an entrepreneur. They find people just like themselves - potential entrepreneurs - and then nurture and develop them, and then all of a sudden they find they've created their own rival!

If you're an entrepreneur looking for people similar to yourself to mentor, understand that eventually they're probably going to leave, and you can't really have hard feelings about that. I've seen that happen far too often, where people say they want to build leaders, but as soon as someone else *becomes* a leader, they turn pouty and upset about it, which doesn't help anybody. They could have been stronger as a team, the two gyms could have worked together and they could have promoted each other, but instead, bridges were burned.

When you're hiring people, hire them with the understanding that the more power you give them the more independent you can make them, but that if you're building a leader, they might become a leader. If you start treating them badly because they are following your advice and doing well, they're going to leave. Keep them happy, keep them as part of the group, and you should be ok.

20 CREATING A CULTURE

If your message is strong, the culture will self-perpetuate without you even trying. There will be no way that you won't create that culture.

For example, our gym is, to quote Rory Miller, an "emotionally safe place to do physically dangerous things". How do we create and maintain that culture? It starts right when people walk in the door, and I greet them with "Hey, I'm Randy, I don't go by *sensei* or *master*, I just go by *Randy* or *hey you*, I won't remember your name for the first little bit, so you don't have to remember mine either". That immediately sets the tone for how things are at the gym. I am not saying this is what you should do; this is just the way I create the culture in my gym. If you want to be a rigid martial arts school, the first impression (because first impression goes a long way) should be that this is a rigid martial arts school. The initial ways in which someone would notice this is through the way they have to bow when they walk in, tie their outfit properly, and so on.

Set your culture right away. Your culture is part of your message. As soon as that happens (within the first two weeks), people are going to know whether or not they want to be there, and they can bail if it isn't for them. This is why a lot of gyms go with the "free two weeks" method of trial classes (at KPC we still offer a free trial class). That free trial is for people to see if they like the culture, if they fit in. We also make it very clear that if you don't fit in at our gym, we won't train you. We are luckily at the position now where we don't need every single person's dollar. Obviously, more is better, but we don't have to train people we don't want to train. For the first little bit this ended up in talks where I would say "hey look, you don't really belong here, this isn't going to work out for you", and then I would recommend other gyms where they would probably fit in a little bit better. By tightening up the way we presented ourselves, these days those people just tend to weed themselves out. We start with a three-month introductory class, where people can come and there's no real upsell, it's just three months of playing with people and they can see if they like it. If they like it, they tend to keep training. This sort of thing creates your culture and your brand, and really attracts the people that want to be there.

While having a strong and consistent culture is very important, it should still represent you and what you are trying to build. Don't do what you think you should do - people see through that very quickly. Do what you want to do, create the space you want, give people the experience you want them to have. They should know what they are getting into already, from your advertising and content creation. If they have bought into what you are selling, and have come to train, and like what is happening, then they are yours to lose.

You need to make sure that you deliver on what you promised, and that everything lines up with what they understand the culture to be, otherwise you lose people. When I was traveling around from gym to gym looking for a place to train, I honestly never really cared what the instructors said about themselves - it was their job to sell to me! Instead, I always asked two simple questions: how long have you been open, and how long has your longest student trained with you. This was a quick way for me to know the level of the instructor, and if what they were saying was true. If they had been open for nine years in the same location, and no one had been with them longer than six months, then that was a big red flag. It showed me that what they were saying did not line up with their reality. People leave when they are not getting what they want (or when you're just a dildo).

There are many ways to create a culture. Starbucks created the "third space" concept, where they made their shops very inviting so people could just hang out, like at home or work (home and work being the first two spaces). With services, you want to build relationships with your clients, get them together, have some fun. A great way for this is with social events. You've probably heard this a thousand times, but I'm going to say it again - you need to have events where people can come together. This is especially true in our gym. I would say, out of our core group of people, three or four of them are extreme introverts, that really had nowhere else to go. They were allowed to be their introverted selves at KPC, they were allowed to do their thing, and to come to events and not get harassed (well, not at first!).

Be a business of your word. Know your message and your demographic. Know your strengths, and what your vision looks like, and stick to that. Throw a party every once in a while! You will get groups of people that want to stay with you for a very long time. This is the best way to create a culture. Trust is the basis of all business, so make sure that you are renewing the clients' faith and trust in you often.

21 KEEP GROWING

All right, that's it! That's my book!

Hopefully all this stuff will help you out, but I want to leave one final note with you. Now that you've got this book, now that you have the skills, the tools, the ability to make your business grow bigger and better than it ever has been, I want you to keep learning. Keep evolving. Keep learning in all aspects of this. Make your *kung fu* strong. Make sure that you're constantly training, you're constantly going to seminars. Make sure you're improving, learning how to network, learning how to sell better. Take an online marketing course, go read everything that Facebook tells you about advertising. Stay in the loop of all the upcoming and updated things, stay on top of your research. Make sure that you're constantly growing and evolving as a human being and as an instructor, because you'd be amazed at how things interconnect. You could be reading a book on how to design websites and have an epiphany about training.

Keep getting those books, keep reading. Look for our stuff! I won't be putting out another book on marketing any time soon (the next book I'm bringing out will be self-defense and self-defense theories from Randy King, tentatively titled "Still Ranting") but I want you to succeed and grow. I want you to keep challenging yourself, and keep learning new skills and new things. If you're a striking coach, take a *jiujitsu* class. If you're a *jiujitsu* guy, take a striking class. If you think you're bad at sales, go to Toastmasters. Keep constantly improving.

Darwin's theory of evolution is often described as the "survival of the fittest" - but really, it's survival of the most <u>adaptable</u>. You can't adapt properly if you don't have enough information to work with.

Pokémon Go, you may remember, was a huge fad. You may think, who cares? Let the hipsters play their weird games! Understand that there are businesses that looked at the Pokémon Go phenomenon and said "how can we make money off this?". Sales at Pokémon lure sites (a lure was a way to attract Pokémon to a certain real-life location) went through the roof. Owners were using lures to attract real people to their businesses. We at KPC even put together a marketing plan to take advantage of the Pokémon fad - we never got the chance to put into action, as the craze died out very quickly - but the point is, if you stay on the forefront of this stuff, if you stay informed, if you're constantly training and constantly learning, staying in shape and reading books, keeping those facts up and stable, you're just going to be a more dynamic and adaptable business. The most adaptable survive.

So now that you've read my book, I think we can be friends! Feel free to add me on Facebook: Randy King[20] (the Edmonton, Alberta one). Please follow me on all the socials, Randy King Live, KPC Self Defense ... some combination of those names will help you find our social media accounts across all the various platforms. I would love to hear from each and every one of you!

On that note, if you have success stories, I'd like to hear about them. If you have further or specific questions, contact me. I am available for private consulting, although, this should be all the stuff you need! I don't think this is rocket science, just information

---

[20] https://www.facebook.com/randy.king.520

that isn't normally presented in a way useful to people in our business. Use it!

Finally, if you want to send me a super-special thank you, you can book me for a self-defense seminar or lecture at your now-growing business.

Keep growing, keep evolving, and get in contact!
Now beat it, I am done with you.

Randy

FURTHER READING

Ferriss, Timothy. *The 4-hour Work Week: Escape the 9-5, Live Anywhere and Join the New Rich.* Random House, 2011.

Fletcher, Aaron N. *Stand Out: A Simple and Effective Online Marketing Plan for Your Small Business.* Turner, 2013.

Gunelius, Susan. *30-minute Social Media Marketing.* McGraw-Hill Education, 2010.

Hayden, C. J. *Get Clients Now! (TM): A 28-Day Marketing Program for Professionals, Consultants, and Coaches.* AMACOM, 2013.

Ries, Al, and Trout, Jack. *The 22 Immutable Laws of Marketing: Violate Them at Your Own Risk.* HarperBusiness, 1994.

Vaynerchuk, Gary. *Jab, Jab, Jab, Right Hook: How to Tell Your Story in a Noisy, Social World.* Harper Collins, 2013.

ABOUT THE AUTHOR

Randy King is a leader in modern-day, realistic self-defense methods that include all of the different aspects of self-defense (e.g. conflict resolution, legal ramifications, internal ethical conflicts, etc.) and not just the fight itself. He is dedicated to passing on the most up-to-date and highly researched methods of self-defense to martial artists and civilians alike, using a combination of Rory Miller's Conflict Communication program, his own hands-on counter ambush and realistic knife defense programs, and his wealth of experience dealing with aggression and weapons.

Randy worked as a doorman for eleven years, and is currently the owner and head coach of KPC Self Defense in Edmonton, Alberta, Canada. He has a wide range of experience in many forms of martial arts, and prides himself on instructing and helping others achieve their fitness and self-defense goals.

Made in the USA
Charleston, SC
18 January 2017